THE GREAT FIRE

Chicago 1871

THE GREAT FIRE
CHICAGO 1871

by Herman Kogan and Robert Cromie

G. P. Putnam's Sons, New York

Contents

Foreword and acknowledgments

In gathering pictorial materials for this centennial history of Chicago's Great Fire of October 8–10, 1871, we were soon struck by a perplexing—and quite frustrating—fact: Nowhere, among either official or unofficial sources we scoured all over the country, is there to be found even one photograph of anything that occurred during those awful hours.

Photographs of ruins and reconstruction abound, but the mystery of the lack of on-the-spot photography persists and leads to conjecture. Was photographic equipment not advanced enough technically to be used in the intense heat? Were photographers in the fire zone too terror-stricken to set up their cameras for even a single shot? Or, as may be most likely, were photographs that were taken destroyed in the holocaust or lost among the frenzied crowds fleeing toward Lake Michigan?

In any case, we have chosen, from among many hundreds of drawings, sketches, paintings, woodcuts and panels from dioramas and cycloramas, scenes depicting events of those frenzied hours. Our selection constitutes, we hope, a vivid pictorial account of what happened in that relatively brief but horrible period in the city's lifetime. Photographs and other illustrative materials of Chicago just before the Great Fire, of the fire ruins and of the city in the period of reconstruction came from a variety of sources.

A number of people gave us valued aid and counsel in our quest.

Primary among them were various members of the Chicago Fire Department: Chief Fire Marshal Curtis Volkamer, Captain Harry G. Maker, Lieutenants Martin Harlow and Martin Lowery and Fireman Kenneth Little, whose knowledge of department history, lore and legend is impressively monumental. We are grateful, too, to Mildred Bruder and Harold Teitlebaum of the Chicago Public Library, to Mary Frances Rhymer and Bernard Szaligowski of the Chicago Historical Society, to Howard F. Rissler of the Illinois State Historical Society and to the staff of the pictorial division of the Library of Congress. Among newspaper colleagues, most helpful were William Winek, Robert Langer and William Sannwald of the newspaper division of Field Enterprises, Inc., publisher of the Chicago *Sun-Times* and the Chicago *Daily News*, Eugene Powers and Patrick Wilson of the Chicago *Tribune* and Anthony C. Berardi and A. G. Wykel of *Chicago Today*.

HERMAN KOGAN
ROBERT CROMIE

"This is the rich and voluptuous city . . .
The Queen of the North and the West!"

In the autumn of 1871, Chicago was a city of 334,000, partly a metropolis and partly a frontier town, 6 miles long and 3 miles wide. Thirteen major railroad lines came into it, and there was heavy traffic both along the Illinois and Michigan Canal and in from Lake Michigan on its eastern border. It was known by various nicknames: Gem of the Prairie, Garden City, Queen City. And some considered it one of the wickedest cities in the land. No one thought to call it the Matchbox, with its thousands of wooden structures, wooden sidewalks and heavy streets paved with wooden blocks.

Chicago was divided into three divisions by its river, which was spanned by a dozen wooden bridges and which forked half a mile west of the lake, one branch running northwest and the other south. Nestling between the lake and the southern branch was the South Division, where the city's extremes of wealth and squalor were represented, the elegant houses along Michigan Avenue contrasting with the hovels of Conley's Patch and Healy Slough and Kilgubbin, the principal business establishments balanced by ramshackle barns and storage sheds. Between the north branch and the lake was the North Division, primarily an area of upper-middle-class and wealthy homes, although along the river stood grain elevators, the Chicago and Northwestern Railroad depot, the McCormick Reaper Works, the wholesale meat market and laborers' dwellings. To the west of the river's fork was the West Division, comprising industrial plants, hundreds of frame houses occupied by workers' families and a small, handsome residential area around Union Park.

More than 600 fires beset Chicago in 1870, and most of them began in barns, despite a city ordinance forbidding the use of lamps or candles, unless enclosed in lanterns, when lighted in places where hay or straw was stored. "Chicago is a city of everlasting pine, shingles, shams, veneers, stucco and putty," warned the *Tribune*. But most citizens disregarded the prospects of calamity as blithely as they did the sermons of ministers inveighing against the high crime rate, political corruption, the universal lust for riches and assorted civic evils. They doted, instead, on the sentiments expressed by Will Carleton, a local poet, who sang of the lusty town:

> This is the rich and voluptuous city,
> The beauty-thronged, mansion-decked city,
> The golden-crowned, glorious Chicago,
> The Queen of the North and the West!

Virtually in the center of the city, at Clark and Randolph streets, stood the ungainly structure that housed the Cook County Courthouse and Chicago's City Hall. The central portion, mainly of wood, had gone up in 1853, two decades after Chicago's incorporation as a town. Five years later it was enlarged by the addition of two flanking wings made of limestone. A contemporary guidebook called the building "one of the homeliest of its kind in the country." The two-story tower in the center held a 5½-ton bell, as well as an outside walk for a watchman whose duty it was to scan the city's skies nightly for signs of fire. The cupola housed a four-faced clock, installed in the spring of 1871, which Chicagoans all over town used to check the correct time. In the west wing were the offices of the mayor, the Board of Police, the chief fire marshal, the fire-telegraph alarm and other city departments. The east wing housed county courtrooms, records and, in the basement, cells of the county jail. The structure, invariably called by Chicagoans the Courthouse, was considered absolutely fireproof, despite the tower and cornices of wood. In this photograph, Clark Street is at the left, Randolph Street runs perpendicularly, with a young man standing at the intersection near the horsecar tracks.

Most popular place for residents and visitors to get a view on clear days of Chicago was from the cupola of the Courthouse. This is toward the northwest, with the Young Men's Association Library, a book bindery and Metropolitan Hall in the foreground. The last, at La Salle and Randolph streets, had for nearly three decades served as a gathering place for various functions ranging from fairs and balls to a memorable sporting event in which John McDevitt, greatest of the local billiard sharks, defeated a rival in a 1,500-point game by running off 1,457 points in a row. To the upper left, practically invisible here, was a bucolic section in the North Division in which lived German truck farmers and, beyond it, the suburb of Lake View, dotted with a few large residences.

Colonel J. H. Wood's famous museum (20,000 curiosities) can be seen to the left in this view east and northeast from the Courthouse roof. This museum and theater, founded in 1863 with exhibits obtained through the purchase of the St. Louis museum, offered awed Chicagoans a chance to view, among other things, "the Zeuglodon, a fossil relic of prehistoric times, which extended its ninety-six feet of bony length to thousands of wondering eyes," Lincoln's catafalque and the Hall of Paintings, one of the largest of which depicted the murder of Jane McRae, near Fort Edward, New York, by Indians who had been chosen to escort her on a journey. In a critique of this work the *Tribune*'s art expert said that the drawing and anatomy of some of the Indians were poorly done, but he expressed high approval of "the marble and moonlight beauty of the slaughtered maiden." It cost patrons only 25 cents to inspect the various curiosities, including the Zeuglodon and the late Miss McRae, but if they wished to view a panorama of the City of London another 15 cents was demanded. Colonel Wood, who took over the management five months after the museum opened, established the theater on a paying basis by bringing in a stock company. Wood relinquished the management in 1868, but returned again in June, 1871.

Anyone gazing north-northeast from the Courthouse could see an interesting mélange. In the immediate foreground, across from the Courthouse, is the Sherman House, one of the largest and finest hostelries in the Midwest, yet west of this hotel along Randolph Street was a row of tumbledown shacks— some built even before the city's official incorporation in 1833—with saloons on the ground floor and lawyers' offices above. Directly north there were still enough patches of trees and grass to justify the comment of a contemporary reporter, Frederick Francis

Cook: "What we now behold is a magnificent natural forest in the midst of a city—or is it not better to say that the city here plays hide and seek in the forest?" Off to the right not far from the lakeshore, mansions were sprouting for families who lived in what a London *Daily News* writer described as "all the graciousness and repose of an old aristocracy." Residents in the North Division did have occasional difficulty getting to their homes in time for dinner because of delays caused by drawbridges that were opened to handle heavy river traffic.

East to the lake was this mixture of wood and stone, mostly business houses. Directly east was Dearborn Street, rapidly becoming a center for the city's newspapers, and a block east was State Street, once a grubby, mud-filled avenue but now developing into the "Street of Merchants" as various companies began a move from Lake Street, for nearly thirty years the primary thoroughfare for such enterprises.

Chicago Historical Society

On a cloudless day, a viewer atop the Courthouse could see as far as the city limits at Thirty-ninth Street, glimpsing perhaps the Gothic building established by Stephen A. Douglas in the early 1850's for his University of Chicago at Thirty-fourth Street and Cottage Grove Avenue or remnants of stockades for Confederate prisoners during the Civil War. A mile or more to the west were the busy Union Stockyards, sending their stench into the crowded wooden jungle of adjoining Bridgeport. Closer to the Courthouse was South Clark Street with the inevitable business houses. In the sector of the South Division below Madison Street and from the lake to the river there was hardly a street without brothels, groggeries, gambling houses or hangouts for thugs and robbers. So high was the crime rate and so frequent were depredations of all sorts that a Chicago *Journal* editorialist wailed, "We are beset on every side by a gang of desperate villains!"

Chicago Historical Society

15

Conley's Patch, the slum sector along lower Fifth Avenue, was a neighborhood comprised of cheap saloons, pawnshops, brothels, one-story shacks and unappealing boardinghouses. The area was very ugly but hardly dull. Early in 1871, for example, the police were called to Ramrod Hall, a single-story structure on Quincy Street, reputed to be the most disreputable bagnio in town. It was run by a woman named Katie Hawkins, who used a horsewhip to keep her thirty to sixty girl employees tractable. But when Katie tried to prevent one of the girls from leaving to get married, "a very lucrative piece of furniture" named Mary Woods, all of Mary's friends came to her aid. The result: a violent free-for-all.

Chicago Today

Terrace Row, which had an unobstructed view of the lake from Michigan Avenue, far enough below the business section to escape the hurly-burly, was probably the town's most elegant residential block. The row consisted of a long stone structure of eleven separate dwellings on the avenue north of Congress Street. Its residents, among the wealthiest in the city, included William Lloyd "Deacon" Bross, part owner of the *Tribune*, and Jonathan Young Scammon, the banker, who later became a newspaper publisher. Bross, a native of Sussex County, New Jersey, came to Chicago in 1848 as a bookseller. Scammon, born in Whitefield, Maine, arrived in 1835, became a founder of the Chicago Historical Society, the Chicago Academy of Sciences and the Chicago Astronomical Society, and contributed $30,000 to build the Fort Dearborn Observatory, which housed the most powerful telescope then in the West.

A rare view of Michigan Avenue, extending north
from Congress Street, showing Terrace Row and the
promenade beyond the low fence next to the lake park
adjoining the lagoon, with the Illinois Central Railroad
embankment to the east. Far in the background are two
grain elevators. Chicago was a leader in the grain trade,
handling 60,000,000 bushels in 1870. These steam-
operated elevators were an innovation. Trains and ships
came up to the side, grain was pumped from them into
large bins and poured out into other cars and vessels
waiting on the opposite side of the elevator.

The Bowen House, at the corner of Michigan Avenue and Monroe Street, was typical of the rather ornate dwellings in the South Division, most of which were shaded by trees and fronted by iron fences and balustrades. Three well-known brothers lived here: James H. Bowen, president of the Third National Bank; George S. Bowen, vice-president of the Young Men's Christian Association; and Chauncey T. Bowen, alderman of the First Ward in 1871.

More of the leisurely charm of what is now one of Chicago's busiest thoroughfares is discernible in this leafy view of Michigan Avenue looking north from Adams Street. The house in the foreground, with the New Orleans-style balconies, was that of Henry Hamilton Honore, a noted Chicago merchant, and at the far end of the block was the William H. Brown mansion, where Abraham Lincoln and his wife were entertained before Lincoln's inauguration in 1861. Honore was an extremely popular citizen, of whom a local admirer once composed this lavish description: "To say that in adversity and in prosperity alike he was ever approachable, genial, courteous, tells not of the extreme kindliness of his eye, the heartiness of his grasp nor of the almost boyish enthusiasm of his address."

Kaufmann & Fabry Company

Michigan Avenue is surprisingly deserted in this photograph of Dearborn Park, looking northeast probably from the roof of one of the buildings on Washington Street. The Illinois Central Railroad yards are in the background, just beyond the Pullman Palace Car Company building. George M. Pullman, who was born in New York State in 1831, came to Chicago to work as a house raiser and in 1859 signed a contract with the Chicago and Alton Railroad to remodel two old passenger cars into sleeping coaches. Four years later he built a new kind of car, which combined day coach and sleeping coach facilities. He next persuaded the Michigan Central Railroad to use these cars, and other lines quickly followed suit.

There is an old-world quality to this idyllic sketch of the Michigan Avenue lakefront, with strolling couples, tiny sail and rowboats, and another of the ever-present trains, drawn by a locomotive with its bell-shaped stack, puffing its way to some distant destination. Ships' masts locate the river for the sharp-eyed. And even then the smokestacks were warning of pollution.

More of the fine houses that lined upper Michigan Avenue toward the southern rim of the North Division. Although this was the city's newest upper-class residential district, with houses that boasted marble façades and mansard roofs, not more than half a mile to the west were workmen's cottages, designed like boxes and uniform in appearance.

This was considered a beautiful building in 1871. It was the Drake-Farwell Block on Wabash Avenue, and one of its most important tenants was the Lyon and Healy music store. The owners were John B. Drake, also proprietor of the Tremont House, and two brothers, Charles Benjamin Farwell and John Villiers Farwell, of the firm of J. V. Farwell and Company. The Farwells were born on a farm in New York State and came to Illinois in 1838. In the mid-1840's both reached Chicago, where Charles went into banking and his brother into the dry goods business. John V. Farwell was a member of the syndicate which built the State Capitol at Austin, Texas, and was one of Chicago's civic leaders.

Chicago was famous throughout the nation for the quality of its hotels, and among the best of these was the Palmer House, at the southeast corner of State and Monroe streets, built by Potter Palmer, the city's foremost real estate man, in 1869–70. The Palmer House was eight stories high, counting the three-story mansard roof, and boasted an unusual safety precaution —fire hoses on every floor. The hotel had 225 rooms and cost $200,-000 to build and another $100,000 to furnish. The Palmer House was opened for business on September 26, 1870, with W. F. P. Meserve as its first manager.

Fred Townsend Collection

Chicago Historical Society

In 1865 the Stewart House, at the northwest corner of State and Washington streets, was remodeled and its name changed to the Merchants' Hotel. This was destroyed by fire in 1867, but rebuilt the same year and opened in January, 1868, as the St. James. It was sold a few months later for $75,000.

There was no civic art museum in the Chicago of 1871, but on Washington Street stood such places as Brand's Temple of Art and Mosher's Art Gallery, shown here along with the offices of T. W. Brophy, a dentist; the Nonotuck Silk Company; and the Liston Collar Company. Brand's establishment displayed mostly lithographs, steel engravings, enlarged photographs, India ink drawings and photographs, in black and white or colors, on porcelain. Mosher's place was actually a photographic studio maintained by Charles D. Mosher, who later photographed all of the city's leading citizens and contributed the pictures to the Chicago Historical Society. Artistic interests did not run high in this community. "Art and mammon," was the *Tribune*'s wry editorial explanation, "are incompatible." The town's leading painter was George P. A. Healy, whose most notable contributions to culture were full-size portraits of civic leaders and rich citizens, and its major sculptor was Leonard W. Volk, whose subjects included Abraham Lincoln in his pre-Presidential days and Stephen A. Douglas.

Crosby's Opera House was on Washington Street, next door to the St. James Hotel and built, to quote a contemporary account, "on a scale of magnificence and beauty not hitherto attempted in this country." To get ideas for his entertainment palace, Uranus H. Crosby, a millionaire liquor distiller, traveled with the architect William W. Boyington to many cities. It was finished in 1865 at a cost of $600,000, but its official opening, scheduled for April 17, was delayed by the assassination three days earlier of President Abraham Lincoln. Albert Crosby, the original owner's brother, was in charge in 1871, and he closed it for the summer for extensive alterations. Some $80,000 was spent on new carpets, bronzes and ornate mirrors for a grand reopening scheduled for Monday, October 9. Theodore Thomas' symphony orchestra was to start a ten-day series of concerts that night. Tickets had sold well, and a capacity crowd was assured for the first performance.

The interior of Crosby's Opera House indicates why it was considered the city's most magnificent entertainment hall, with its profusion of draperies, painted ceilings and intricate carvings. This drawing depicts a concert audience, but the theater was used for other events. In 1868 the Republicans held their Presidential convention here, nominating the Civil War's Northern hero, General Ulysses S. Grant.

No free public libraries were available, but there were sixty-eight bookstores ranging from general emporiums to those specializing in foreign language publications or religious literature. This is Booksellers' Row on State Street between Washington and Madison streets, whose tenants included the Western News Company, the publishing houses of A. S. Barnes and S. C. Griggs, and W. B. Keen and Cooke and Company. Even as a relatively young city, Chicago was a publishing center not only for books but for magazines. Two of the most popular with women were Martha Louise Rayne's *Chicago Magazine of Fashion, Music and Home Reading,* which contained articles dealing with latest styles and "cultural pursuits" and lithographs of Parisian fashions in full color. Many magazines were available for children, the most popular among them the *Little Corporal,* which always carried stories advising its young readers that if they wished to emulate heroes of such tales, they were not to swear, lie, tattle, disobey their teachers and parents or chew tobacco.

Chicago Today

Another view of Booksellers' Row from across the street. The lion's head at the lower right of the photograph is that of the sculptured beast in front of the Charles Gossage and Company department store on the southwest corner of State and Washington streets. Gossage was British-born, a restless man who ran businesses in South Carolina, Iowa and Ohio before settling in Chicago. One of the first merchants to move from Lake Street to State Street in the 1860's, he, like his competitors, subsidized Mrs. Rayne's magazine with hefty advertising.

The businessmen's shift to State Street was touched off by the sagacious Potter Palmer, who bought up a lot of frontage along the avenue, compelled the authorities to institute improvements and then built, at State and Washington streets, the city's largest department store. The building, seen here, was known as Palmer's Marble Palace, and Palmer rented it for $50,000 a year to Marshall Field and Levi Z. Leiter, rapidly becoming the city's prime merchants. Field, after arriving in Chicago from Pittsfield, Massachusetts, in 1856, had clerked in the Cooley and Wadsworth dry goods store, saved his money and invested carefully and wisely. He and Leiter, the firm's bookkeeper, formed a partnership in a Lake Street store in 1863. Five years later they assumed full management of the State Street store. By 1871 their stock and furnishings were valued at more than $3,000,000.

Kogan-Wendt Collection

Palmer's campaign to modernize State Street was still in progress when this photograph was taken early in 1871. He got the authorities to widen the street to 27 feet, lay new gas, sewer and water pipes and replace some of the wooden blocks. He himself contracted for the building of no fewer than thirty commercial buildings along a 2-mile stretch. At the north end there was still a mixture of small businesses—tailorshops, spice stores, cheap lodging houses. Horsecars, called bobtails, ran on a single track and often jumped the track into the mud.

The Honore Block, extending along Dearborn Street north from Adams Street to Monroe Street, was one of the city's finest office buildings, with much made in the public prints of its mansard roof of new and elaborate design covered with slate and its Otis steam passenger elevator. "Our citizens interested in this substantial method of construction," stated *The Land Owner* magazine, "will do well to examine it." Henry Hamilton Honore, who built this structure, also owned the Boardman House, considered the only "truly family hotel" in town in the 1860's.

This structure, at the southwest corner of Madison and Clark streets, was largely occupied by insurance firms.

Chicago Historical Society

Despite the shabby appearance of this block—Clark Street south of Madison Street—a close look will reveal three gentlemen in top hats. One is emerging from the premises of P. F. Logan, importer and dealer in wines, brandies and cigars, but the other two stand improbably in front of A. Lipman's pawnshop. The block is a bustling one. Available are a steam printer, bookbindery, tailor and draper, billiards room (in the basement in midblock behind the first wagon), a seller of trusses, a surgeon whose specialty is eye and ear surgery, a justice of the peace, a maker of hoopskirts and a seller of boots and shoes.

Chicagoans always have loved trees. This leafy vista extended west along Washington Street from State Street.

Marshall Field Archives

Chicago Historical Society

The Tremont House, at Lake and Dearborn streets, was built by James and Ira Couch, former tailors, in 1850, after two earlier Tremont Houses had burned down. It was once known as Couch's Folly because few outsiders believed enough guests could be found to fill its five floors of rooms and repay the $75,000 it cost to erect. The Tremont was the first major building in town to be lighted with gas, and the *Gem of the Prairie* described it as one of the city's "chief orna-ments" and said there was "no hotel in the Union superior to it in any respect." In 1858, on consecutive evenings, Abraham Lincoln and Stephen Douglas spoke from the Tremont's balconies, and Ralph Waldo Emerson stayed there during a lecture tour. Douglas died at the hotel in 1861. The Tremont was a favorite with travelers, since it was within walking distance of the huge Union depot and had a Michigan Central Railroad ticket office on the ground floor.

Chicago Historical Society

Chicago Historical Society

This group on the third-floor balcony of the Tremont House includes George Francis Train, well-known world traveler, author and lecturer from New York City, who made a memorable prophecy during his speech in Farwell Hall, Madison and Clark streets, on Saturday evening, October 7, 1871. Train, the hatless gentleman in the front row, told his listeners: "This is the last public address that will be delivered within these walls! A terrible calamity is impending over the City of Chicago! More I cannot say; more I dare not utter."

The circus seems to have been in town when this rare print of the Sherman House at Clark and Randolph streets was made, although curiously enough the artists, Otto Jevne and Peter M. Almini, appear to have forgotten to show anyone peering from his hotel room window at the passing spectacle which included knights in armor, an elephant and at least a couple of dromedaries. The Sherman House, built in 1861, afforded patrons a superb view of the city from its railed observation tower on the roof, six stories above the street, and of the bustling intersection from a second-story promenade balcony.

The merchants' move to State Street was gradual rather than abrupt, and Lake Street in the autumn of 1871 was still the primary avenue for shoppers of all kinds. In this photograph, one can detect a sign, "Rare Books," far down on the left side, and there are also shops for hats, caps and furs, dry goods and carpets, watches and jewelry. The street was bursting with shops, stores and wholesale warehouses—and teeming with stevedores, sidewalk peddlers and fishmongers. On hot days the stench from the river was formidable, and on wet days mud spurted from between the wooden paving blocks. Property values here were higher than just about anyplace in the city: $2,000 a front foot.

There is something reminiscent of a Whistler etching in the photographic study, top, of the South Branch of the Chicago River on what seems to have been a faintly misty day, with half a dozen tall-masted ships and the middle-pivot bridges at Lake, Randolph and Madison streets. Bottom, the river again, looking westward from Rush Street. And again, a forest of masts.

The city's Water Tower of neomedieval Gothic design and the pumping station were built in 1867 for $2,500,000 and stood on opposite sides of Pine Street (now Michigan Avenue) at Chicago Avenue. Water came through a 2-mile tunnel from Lake Michigan to the east, then was supplied from this system to 154 miles of pipe stretching throughout the city. Until then it had not been unusual for little fish to come wriggling through kitchen taps because of the city's inefficient system of wells and reservoirs. Improvement was so great with the advent of the waterworks that one local writer, Franc B. Wilkie, was moved to quip: "The cleansing properties of the new water are wonderful. Children whose faces have been washed in it have been lost and never found. Their mothers cannot recognize them."

Chicago Historical Society

In contrast with Michigan Avenue, where much of the living was of an almost jowl-to-jowl or wall-to-wall type—even in the case of such high-style examples as Terrace Row—was the North Division, where the neighborhood retained a small-town atmosphere in which those who could afford it took half a block, or sometimes the whole block, on which to build. An example is the George Rumsey residence at Cass (now Wabash Avenue) and Huron streets, with its slim colonnades, its roomy porch and balconies. This occupied a quarter of a block and stood across the street from St. James' Episcopal Church, one of the city's most fashionable.

The home of Ezra B. McCagg was another showplace in the North Division at Clark and White (now Delaware Place) streets, opposite Washington Square, one of the city's first public parks. McCagg, a lawyer and partner of Jonathan Scammon, was an art collector and bibliophile whose library was one of the Midwest's finest. It contained, among many rare volumes, writings and letters of Jesuits and other early settlers in the Northwest Territory.

Wabash Avenue at Peck Court. One of the quieter residential areas of the city, some blocks north of the business section.

45

One of the city's largest parks was Lincoln Park in the North Division, whose lagoon, also known as Swan Lake, was a favorite trysting place. Ezra McCagg was among a group of prominent citizens who went to the state legislature in Springfield in 1869 and obtained authorization for the expenditure of funds to create this park and several others in the South and West Divisions. This was thirty-one years after the city's first park, Dearborn, was laid out at Michigan Avenue and Washington Street.

"No clouds, no stars, nothing else but fire. . . ."

Chicago Historical Society

The summer of 1871 had been an unusually dry one in Chicago. Only five inches of rain fell between July and October, and even this amount was rationed into a small number of showers. The rainfall in the month preceding October 8 had been less than one inch. In addition, some twenty-seven fires struck during the first week of that month, culminating on Saturday night, October 7, in a blaze which broke out in a planing mill on the West Side and devoured virtually every building in a four-block area before it was brought under control on Sunday morning. One person died and several were injured, and there was also the loss of hose and other fire-fighting equipment, including one of the city's seventeen steam fire engines and a hose cart. Nearly half of the city's 185 firemen fought this fire, and many remained on duty all day Sunday as embers still smoldered. Scores of firemen were tired to the point of collapse that Sunday, their eyes red and swollen from smoke and cinders. The *Tribune,* in a story about the Saturday night fire, sounded a warning almost as ominous as Train's: "For days past alarm has followed alarm, but the comparatively trifling losses have familiarized us to the pealing of the Courthouse bell, and we had forgotten that the absence of rain for three weeks had left everything in so dry and inflammable a condition that a spark might set a fire which could sweep from end to end of the city."

While some still write off the story of the cow and the lantern as at best apocryphal, there is no doubt at all that the Great Fire which destroyed most of Chicago and left 100,000 persons homeless did indeed begin, modestly enough, in the cowshed behind the home of Patrick O'Leary, a laborer, on De Koven Street. O'Leary bought the property in 1864 for $500 and at the time of the fire had rented the front portion to Patrick McLaughlin, a railroad man. The O'Learys, on the Sunday evening of October 8, had retired early in their own quarters, which were immediately behind those of the McLaughlins, and seem to have been undisturbed by the fact that the McLaughlins were having a family party in honor of Mrs. McLaughlin's brother, newly arrived from Ireland. But a neighbor, Daniel "Pegleg" Sullivan, a drayman, was enjoying the sound of McLaughlin's fiddle as Sullivan sat on the boardwalk across the street, leaning against a wooden fence in the warm October night. Suddenly Sullivan saw a flicker of flame from the barn at the rear of the O'Leary lot, some 90 feet or so from the street. He scrambled awkwardly upright and hobbled rapidly toward the barn, meanwhile shouting, "Fire! Fire! Fire!" at the top of his lungs.

Despite Sullivan's later testimony, which stated that when he passed the O'Leary place, there were no lights inside and that he managed to save one half-grown calf from the flaming stable occupied only by several cows and a horse as he entered, this is the typical contemporary artist's version of how the fire that destroyed Chicago began. Perhaps it is not quite typical, since it portrays Mrs. O'Leary as more human and a lot less witchlike than do those on the opposite page. As is evident, however, the cow has just flicked the lamp over with a careless hoof, and Mrs. O'Leary is frozen in terror. The original drawing was identified as showing "the cause of the Great Chicago Fire" and bore beneath it the subtitle: "A warning to all who use kerosene lamps."

In this highly imaginative and exaggerated painting by L. V. H. Crosby, the famous cow is spotted, and the artist's notion that Mrs. O'Leary was an obviously evil character is shown not only by the face he has given her but also by the rats and a ghostly-looking cat. This sketch later appeared in a magazine, along with Mrs. O'Leary's supposedly irate reaction to it and an Irish-dialect poem by a wisely anonymous bard quoting her as blaming neither the cow nor herself but Crosby. If Crosby had not been in the barn, wrote the smart-alecky poet,

Chicago Historical Society

> How else could ye know,
>   I'd a cat and a sow,
> An' illegant chickens —
>   high perchin',
> If yerself had not been,
>   jist afore I coom in,
> Through my barn for rich
>   plunder a searchin'?

W. O. Mull, who perpetrated this drawing, has inserted two black cats, a companion cow, a frenzied dog, an alarmed pig and miscellaneous birds and rats, as Mrs. O'Leary once more goes sprawling and Chicago's fate is sealed. Obviously, no one bothered to talk with Sullivan or Mrs. O'Leary, or even to discover what the inside of the shed was like. An unknown writer in the Chicago *Journal* summed up the lady's predicament rather well:

"Even if it were an absurd rumor, forty miles wide of the truth, it would be useless to attempt to alter 'the verdict of history.' Mrs. O'Leary has made a sworn statement in refutation of the charge, and it is backed by other affidavits; but to little purpose. She is in for it and no mistake. Fame has seized her and appropriated her, name, barn, cows and all. She has won, in spite of herself, what the Ephesian youth panted for."

William Henry Musham was foreman of the Little Giant engine company, whose station was about six blocks from the O'Leary home. He and his men reached the blaze after a tragic initial delay.

When the flames behind the O'Leary place were noticed about 9:30 P.M. by Mathias Schaffer, the watchman on duty on the Courthouse roof, he instructed William J. Brown, the young fire-alarm operator in the office below, to sound the alarm for Box 342. Unfortunately, this was about a mile from the actual fire and so was not heeded by the Little Giant company and another close to where the fire had started. Instead, it brought in companies from many blocks distant and caused further delay because they had to search for the fire that actually was not in the vicinity of Box 342.

Peering more intently into the night at flames shooting ever higher, Schaffer now became aware that he had made a mistake. He ordered Brown to correct it by sounding the alarm for a box closer to the O'Leary place. For a forever-unexplained reason, Brown stubbornly and foolishly refused—and again sent out the wrong signal.

Musham's company on Maxwell Street was finally alerted by Joseph Lagger, the Little Giant's stoker, who saw the burgeoning flames.

The Little Giant, shown here two years after the Great Fire with its crew outside the Maxwell Street quarters. All major Fire Department vehicles had special titles affixed to them—either descriptive nicknames, as in the case of this one and such others as Liberty No. 7, Pioneer Hook and Ladder No. 1 and Tempest Hose No. 1 or names of prominent citizens and Fire Department officials past and present.

Chicago Historical Society

Another bearded hero of the fight was Matthias Benner, one of the Fire Department's three assistant fire marshals. Head of the forces in the West Division where the fire began, Benner had been out late the night before leading the battles against the big West Side blaze. He was at home on Randolph Street when the alarm came. He scrambled into his clothes and hurried to the corner of Randolph and Jefferson streets, where he was picked up by his driver. At once he suggested that the alarm pulled for Box 342 was an error, and he directed his driver to head toward the O'Leary barn. When Benner arrived, Musham and his Little Giant company were already at work. Noticing that a row of buildings, housing groceries and saloons a block away had taken fire, Benner ordered Musham to recruit local residents to man a second line of hose. For a few minutes, the citizens did so, but then they abandoned the hose and fled—thereby preventing a chance to halt the fire in the O'Leary block.

Hose Cart No. 6—typical of the equipment of the time—is depicted speeding to a fire, with two firemen clinging behind.

Chicago Public Library

The Williams, a steam fire engine precisely like the one pictured here outside Engine Co. 17 at 558 West Lake Street, was in its quarters ready to leave on an alarm that later proved to be false when the regular alarm began ringing for Box 342—Schaffer's error compounded by young Brown's refusal to correct it. Since this was not in the Williams' territory for a first alarm, the horses were unhitched and the Williams did not move. This was a dangerous and fatal mistake, for the Williams, the department's newest steamer, could throw 700 gallons of water a minute and, had the proper alarm been turned in immediately, could surely have quelled the flames and kept them from spreading. By the time the error was corrected and the Williams did get to the fire area the blaze was widening.

Chicago Fire Department

The steam fire engine Long John—named for "Long John" Wentworth, a former mayor—played a major role in the Great Fire, although it was handicapped during the latter stages of the losing battle when a well-meaning citizen, finding the Long John's horses tethered to a corner of the Parmelee Stables in the business district of the South Division as the flames drew ever nearer, untied the horses and led them away. The Long John, which had been pouring water into the Grand Pacific Hotel, had to be pulled by hand the rest of the time it was used to battle flames.

Pioneer Hook and Ladder used during the fire. Note rear driver and buckets hanging underneath the ladders.

Chicago Fire Department

Chicago Fire Department

Hose elevator company and
equipment used to fight the flames.
A rare photograph taken late in
1871.

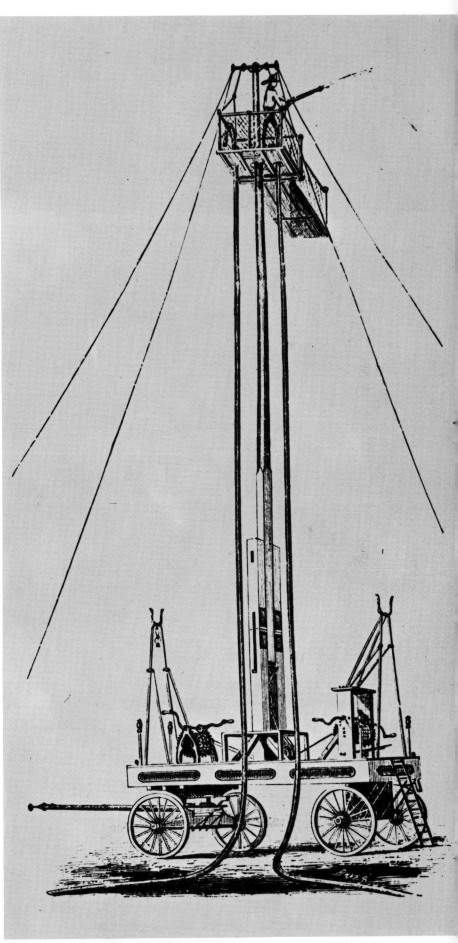

Drawing showing hose elevator
employed in rescue work and reaching the flames in areas inaccessible
from the ground.

Fire Marshal Robert A. Williams, the man in charge. Williams, who had directed the Saturday night struggle against the fire that burned over several blocks on the West Side and left the department worn out and short of equipment, was asleep when the first alarm sounded in his bedroom. His wife's elbow helped jar him awake, and a moment after he was dressed and on the street, his wagon came rattling up. From then on until the battle was over, Williams played the part of a skillful general, commanding outgunned and outnumbered troops, whose only chance was to fight as long as a position was tenable and then to conduct a series of strategic re-treats. The fire's head start, the tinder-dry city, the high wind and the tremendous number of highly inflammable wooden buildings throughout Chicago were too much of a handicap for anyone to overcome. Williams, a native of Canada, was forty-five years old. He had joined the department in 1848 and rose through the ranks to become chief marshal. He was six feet tall, sturdily built and seemingly tireless. Neighbors reported, with admiration, that he always reached the street in front of his home within two or three minutes of a night alarm and sometimes responded to two or more such alarms during the same dusk-to-dawn period.

In the West Division, firemen fight on. Note the metal horn through which the fireman with his hand on a hydrant is shouting directions to someone high above him and, in the burning building to the rear, a man tossing bundles from the window. The flames spread so rapidly, driven by a rising wind, that there was little the firemen could do after the first embers soared beyond De Koven Street. The official account of the fire, given in testimony afterward, tells how Assistant Fire Marshal Benner, coming out of a building at the corner of Jefferson and De Koven streets, met his assistant, John Schank, and was told to rush all available equipment north.

"John," asked Benner in surprise, "where has the fire gone to?"

"She has gone to hell-and-gone," was the reply.

A vivid scene of an area stretching northward from the fire's origin into the hub of the city around the Courthouse. This graphic reconstruction was from the famous Gross Cyclorama, which went on view in 1892 and remained one of the city's most popular attractions for more than a decade. It was housed in a specially built circular structure at Michigan Avenue between Madison and Monroe streets. Nearly 150,000 people came each year to gaze at the half dozen scenes painstakingly created on canvases 50 feet long. A corps of artists used two tons of paints and oils and numbered among their ranks France's Salvador Mege, Paul Wilhelm of Düsseldorf, Richard Lorenze of Munich, England's cyclorama specialist, Edward James Austen, and such Chicago artisans as Oliver Dennett Grove, Ernest Albert and Edgar Cameron, the latter a member of the *Tribune* staff.

Library of Congress

One hazardous escape route some victims were forced to take was the free-fall leap from windows. Many who did so suffered broken legs and arms but escaped death. In the panic some people did inexplicable things, placing more value on possessions than on their lives. One woman on Adams Street was forcibly removed from her burning home not once but three times when she persisted in returning. Despite warning cries, some men were seen to run suddenly into burning buildings for no apparent reason, to be swallowed by bursts of flame even as they reached the doors.

This drawing by an anonymous artist and titled by him "A Family Terribly Perish on the Roof of a House" depicts a scene tragically common during the Great Fire—although the man hiding his eyes might well have been better advised to slide down the rainpipe visible just below the railing on the right. As in scores of other cases, the victim obviously was in panic and unable to think rationally. Thousands of others did, of course, manage to escape from burning buildings, and streets leading away from the fire were constantly jammed with men, women, children and vehicles loaded with goods and furnishings. Some citizens who had seen the early stages of the fire and did not believe it would be serious went home to sleep, only to be routed later. And others who lived farther west and south beyond the fire area actually slept through the holocaust and were astounded to find a good part of the city destroyed when they woke up on Monday morning.

There were drunks, scores of them. Saloons were invaded, and looters grabbed bottles from the shelves or overturned whiskey barrels, whose contents spilled into the streets to mix with the heat and fire and produce thin wavering strands of blue flame that streaked in the gutters toward sewers. Drunken men staggered through the crowds, and women of all ages lurched in the streets, yelling inanities like "Chickey, chickey, craney crow, I went to the well to wash my toe!" or shrilling obscenities. Actually, most of the lurid tales later related in print were without foundation, although robbery, looting and some arson were persistent. Some merchants simply gave their wares away. When prisoners were released from the cells in the Courthouse basement, some immediately headed for nearby saloons or clothing shops, while others were actually welcomed by A. H. Miller, a jeweler across from the Courthouse. Aware that the flames would engulf the area, Miller handed out watches, rings and bracelets to the freed men as they streamed across Randolph Street toward his store.

Two highly imaginative views of what happened during the spreading fire, both from a postfire pamphlet titled *The Horrors of Chicago*. At top, the artist has attempted to record a multitude of events—an arsonist at work, a woman leaping with babe in arms from a building, a looter hanged. At right is an artist's depiction of a lynching. In point of fact, General Philip Sheridan, under whose command the city later was placed during a brief emergency period, wrote, "I am happy to state that no case of outbreak or disorder has been reported. No authenticated case of incendiarism has reached me, and the people of the city are calm, quiet and well-disposed."

The flames, the wind and the noise created infectious panic. This shows Clark and Randolph streets with the fire sweeping close. People fled on foot, on horseback or in carriages, sometimes carrying the young, the ill and the very old. They saved various things, from strongboxes to trunks to puppies, a length of stovepipe, a piece of marble, a basketful of newly washed clothes, a rooster riding on his owner's shoulder, oil paintings, books and—in some cases—the first thing they managed to grab as they ran from home or office. In the background guests are dropping luggage from the Sherman House balcony.

Courthouse Square, at about one thirty Monday morning when the Courthouse roof began to smolder. Forty-five minutes later the bell tower collapsed as the roof fell in. By this time the prisoners had been freed from their basement cells. The murderers were led away under guard, while the others were showered with Miller's gems. From his office across the street a civic-minded gentlemen, John G. Shortall, one of the town's foremost real estate dealers, salvaged valued documents. Aided by a friend, who halted a wagon at gunpoint, Shortall and his employees saved a vast number of abstracts and deed records, which were of supreme importance after the fire because the city's official records of property transactions were destroyed with the Courthouse.

Chicago Historical Society

John R. Chapin, an artist for *Harper's Weekly,* was stopping at the Sherman House and knew nothing of the fire until he heard someone rattling his door some hours after he retired. When no one answered his call, he slept once more and this time was awakened by the noise of footsteps, a commotion in the halls and a strange roaring outside. He opened the shutters and found the city in flames. Chapin dressed quickly, taking his valise and remembering the watch under his pillow, and abandoned the hotel with his fellow guests. He found his way through the Washington Street tunnel to the West Side, aiding a couple of frightened women on the way, then walked north to the

Randolph Street bridge and sketched these refugees fleeing over that span from the South Side to safety in the West Division. A vast grain elevator was ablaze nearby, as was the Nevada Hotel, across the river, at Franklin and Washington streets, a favorite dwelling place for many of the town's newspaper and theatrical folk who were below the top eche-lon. The Briggs House and Peter Schuttler's Wagon Works also were on fire, and as Chapin wrote later, the blaze "was devouring the most stately and massive buildings as though they had been the cardboard playthings of a child. . . . One after another they dissolved, like snow on a mountain."

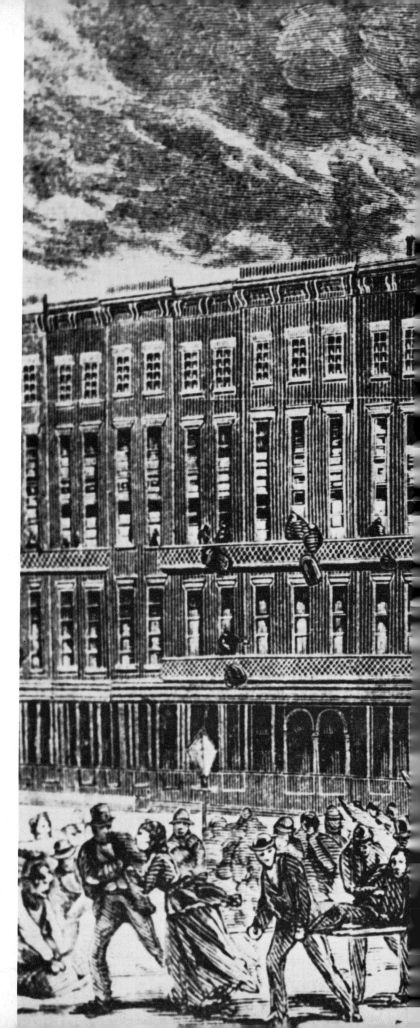

The Tremont House, just as the vanguard of the flames reached it. A couple of steamers may be seen in the mid-foreground, throwing water against the front of the building. It was about 3 A.M. Monday when the Tremont began burning, and since the elevators soon quit working, fleeing guests either ran down the stairs or risked leaping over the banisters. Alexander Frear, a New York politican, was in the Tremont as the fire neared, searching for some relatives. He peered from one of the windows up Dearborn Street where he saw flames that seemed "impelled with the force of a tremendous blow-pipe. Everything that they touched melted." Frear continued his search, kicking in the doors of locked rooms, but his efforts were unsuccessful. He then helped another man carry an insensible woman, very large and laden with jewelry, down to the lobby. There, to his surprise, she regained consciousness and ran out, followed by the other man.

Chicago Today

Battling the blaze on Lake Street are streamers, hose carts and firemen throwing water from ladders, the roof or the ground or running with axes in their hands. Curiously uninvolved are bystanders, possibly those whose homes or businesses are unthreatened, out-of-towners, or ones whose possessions already have gone. One weary fireman, Thomas Byrne, paused in his labors to tell a *Tribune* reporter, "You couldn't see anything over you but fire. . . . No clouds, no stars, nothing else but fire. . . ."

Sometime after one o'clock on Monday morning, John De Koven and George and William Sturges, officers of the North Western Bank in the Chamber of Commerce Building, located on Washington Street in the block directly south of the Courthouse, hurried into the business district from the North Side, suspecting that the bank would burn. They found the building already in danger and the fire moving rapidly against the Courthouse. Inside, the watchman with drawn revolver and a private policeman offered to help. George Sturges worked the vault's combination, which had been set for the letters *OATS,* and said, after his fumbling first attempts, "If my horse were here, he could find oats faster than I can." While they were emptying the vault, a young man, Eben Matthews, who was a clerk in one of the other offices, ran in and asked permission to use the vault for his firm's books. He was allowed to do so, and the others left, running east on Washington Street with their treasure and hiring a hack to drive them to Twentieth Street for $100 in cash. Meanwhile, Matthews, who had single-handedly been trying to save the building, was back in his office when a fireman broke the window and shouted that he had better leave at once. He left.

At Crosby's Opera House virtually everything was ready for the Monday night opening of the Theodore Thomas orchestra. Crosby himself conferred at the building on Sunday with Melville Stone, owner of a foundry, who was to have delivered 1,000 folding chairs early Monday morning so that setting them up would not interfere with the orchestra's rehearsal. George Upton, music critic for the *Tribune,* was also present, inspecting the new decorations. During their conversation someone mentioned that the stage carpenter had lost his home in the Saturday night fire and added that it would indeed

be terrible if the Opera House went. Crosby laughed and said there was no chance. "I have studied the statistics of theater fires," he said, "and they occur on an average of once in five years. We had a fire two years ago, so we are immune for three more." The immunity lasted a somewhat shorter time— roughly eight hours—and when the Thomas orchestra pulled into town Sunday night, the downtown section was lighting the sky. The musicians went on to St. Louis. As Crosby's burned, a music teacher, C. W. Perkins, was forced to leap from the third floor. He suffered only a broken arm.

Chicago Public Library

The use of explosives to blow up buildings in the path of the fire was one of the methods adopted—often with a complete lack of success— to halt the blaze. Here, however, whether by coincidence or because of the explosion, a building probably demolished under the direction of James H. Hildreth, a former alderman, marks the end of the fire's southward march at Wabash Avenue and Congress Street. General Philip Sheridan, who tried to commandeer some powder and conduct his own explosions, was balked by the man left in charge of Hildreth's powder supply. The "very trusty man," named John Mahoney, defied three attempts by Sheridan to take some of the supplies, even when the illustrious Civil War general brought a policeman with him to reinforce the order. At this point Mahoney drew a pistol and threatened to use it.

Chicago Historical Society

Wabash Avenue and Harrison Street, about five o'clock Monday morning. The church at the left is the Wabash Avenue Methodist, at the corner of that intersection, which was twice saved from destruction. The first time its pastor, the Reverend R. M. Hatfield, pleaded that it be spared after Hildreth had already carried five barrels of powder into the basement. The eager explosion maker was overruled by Mark Sheridan, a member of the city's three-man Board of Police, who told him to wait. The second time came when fire broke out in the wooden tower on the northwest corner of the roof, causing Hildreth to remind everyone within reach that he had urged the blowing up of the church to save the rest of the South Side. This fire was extinguished by the daring of a former professional gymnast and Union scout, William Haskell, who made his way to the roof, up the top of the tower and down inside, where he finally quenched the flames with water hauled up in buckets and fed to him by a two-man volunteer bucket brigade, one white, one black. A collection was taken up on the spot by grateful onlookers certain that Haskell had saved everything to the south. But whoever made the collection vanished before the money reached the modest gymnast, who simply went home and neglected to talk about his heroism.

Arthur R. Waud, the renowned Civil War battlefield artist, was in St. Louis with a writer, Ralph Keeler, covering the St. Louis Fair for *Every Saturday* when word reached them of the Great Fire. They immediately headed for the burning city, reaching town by way of the Alton and St. Louis Railroad, and were soon absorbed, as Keeler later wrote, "straightway in the horror and panic of the great disaster." Waud made many on-the-spot pencil drawings, of which this is a striking example. Some thirty others and this one were purchased a decade ago by the Chicago Historical Society from Malcom F. Burns of Millington, New Jersey, Waud's grandson.

84

Chicago Historical Society

"Fleeing from the burning city" is the caption someone—presumably Waud himself—wrote on this study in light and darkness, which suggests most wonderfully the tension of this frozen moment. There is a small child, arm extended to the full as he clings to a coattail, an elderly man carrying an infant, a woman without shoes, residents emerging in haste from dwellings on the left.

A Gross Cyclorama reconstruction of the scene outside the Marine Hospital near the mouth of the Chicago River as flames attacked the structure and drove harried and terrorized patients, doctors and nurses toward the water.

88

These people, unable to run in any other direction, are heading for the protection of the Lake Michigan shore. Many waded into the water up to their chests or buried one another in sand to escape the biting sparks. Some took shelter behind two high walls at Superior Street near the lake, and other managed to get completely out of reach of the flames by walking north along the shore after soaking their clothing with water. This is a Gross Cyclorama panel.

T.M.AVERY LUMBER

Chicago Public Library

90

The rigging of the ships is on fire
in the *Harper's Weekly* illustration
(left) of what conditions were like
on the Chicago River about seven
o'clock Monday morning. Grain
elevators burn in the distance, and
on the dock a frantic civilian, perhaps one whose property is threatened with destruction, is leading a
small group of firemen on the run.
In the drawing above, with the water pouring onto the blazing elevators, there is a genuine nightmarish
quality inherent in a disaster of such
magnitude.

The Gross Cyclorama again, this segment showing the north end of Michigan Avenue with the buildings above Randolph Street, to the east, just starting to go, as the residential blocks on the west, in the upper distance, still await the flames. Note the galloping horses, which could easily have been ones turned loose from some blazing stable.

An unusually vivid Gross Cyclorama panel, with crowds moving across the Rush Street Bridge toward the North Division. Hardly anyone expected that the flames would bound across the river into this section, but within an hour after this mob and others streaming across other bridges had reached what they thought was certain safety, harsh winds hurled burning brands into their midst.

Scene on the prairie, monday ni...

Refugees on the prairies west of the city as Waud saw them sometime Monday night or early Tuesday after the rain began to fall. While the storm, which began in some places by 11 P.M. Monday, brought extra hardships to the homeless, especially to the sick or the very old or very young, it also was badly needed insurance against a rebirth of the fire which, with a shift in the wind, might very well have gained a fresh foothold on the West or far South Sides. Mary Fales, driven from her North Side home hours before, remembered it this way: "I never felt so grateful in my life as to hear the rain pour down."

Throng of refugees on the north side of the river, watching the spectacle of a city's destruction. The fire sailed north over the river by 1:30 A.M. Monday, when embers struck the paint and carpentry shop of Lill's Brewery near Chicago Avenue and the lake. This blaze remained isolated, but an hour or so later the flames struck several other points, including a carload of kerosene on a Northwestern Railroad spur, Wright's Stables, near the State Street Bridge, the bridge itself and the wooden trestle which ran above it. From there —and very quickly—the flames ate their way through wooden houses on a direct line from State Street to the Water Tower.

The lakefront area known as the Sands, north of the river, was a haven for thousands of Chicagoans driven from their homes by the flames. Some arrived carrying or dragging a few possessions. Others brought nothing. Babies were born and old people died within earshot of the adjoining waters. Sometime Monday the heat and shower of sparks became so unbearable that many of those on the Sands, who had even taken to the shallow water near shore for protection, moved onto the lighthouse pier, which was north of the river and ran out into the lake. Among these were members of the family of Edward Ilsley Tinkham, cashier of the Second National Bank, who earlier had loaded some $1,600,000 in money and negotiable securities from the bank into a trunk and brought it home. The Tinkhams found their way to the iron lighthouse at the end of the pier, and a short while later the black coachman Tinkham had hired to guard them and transport the trunk showed up, dragging the treasure behind him. Eventually, after a dangerous trip to the West Side by tug, Tinkham reached safety and promptly entrained for Milwaukee, where he deposited the contents of the trunk in a vault.

Chicago Historical Society

The artist C. S. Reinhart drew this scene, showing
refugees in the streets—a mixture of young and old
and what seems to be rich and poor—or possibly the
formerly rich, now also poor. A man in what appears
to be a nightcap carries two little girls, a woman
comforts either husband or father, and the brave
young lady in the left foreground shows at least as
much composure and defiance of events as the man
leaning on his hands and listening without conviction
to the woman crouched before him.

A panoramic view of the burning city as it looked from the lakefront, near the mouth of the river, was sketched by Waud and appeared in the November 4 issue of *Every Saturday*. He has penciled in the refugees, human and animal, and at least a hint of the personal belongings which those who fled brought with them to the safety of the lake.

101

Chicago *Tribune*

A refugee camp on one of the prairies. When the fire finally ended, except for the coal piles which smoldered for weeks, there were about 100,000 homeless. Some 20,000 of the dispossessed had left town, and another estimated 15,000 were being cared for by friends, which left roughly 65,000 persons in need of shelter. Tents and hastily constructed barracks were pressed into use, but because of a shortage of stoves, only a few of these makeshift lodgings were heated as long as three weeks after the fire. Typhoid and smallpox cases were common, and the papers, by October 16, were warning their readers to boil water before using it.

Outside Chicago itself unscrupulous persons were not above posing as refugees in order to obtain handouts. As a Philadelphia newspaper commented: "Chicago was probably the most populous city in the world previous to the conflagration. Some 14,000,-000 of her 'destitute citizens' have passed through this city in the past three weeks. You can't throw a cat in any direction without hitting a 'sufferer.'"

Another *Harper's Weekly* sketch, this one by Joseph Becker, shows Lincoln Park with refugees camping after the fire. There seems to be plenty of food, even though some grocers had doubled their prices on scarce commodities, and bread, cheese and milk were in short supply. Fresh water went for $5 a barrel, for a while, in areas remote from the lake. Food was rushed in from out of town, but some of the bread reached Chicago spoiled because it had been shipped while still hot. Local upholsterers were making mattresses stuffed with hay, excelsior and cornhusks at the rate of 300 or 400 dozen a day.

EVENING JOURNAL-EXTRA.

CHICAGO, MONDAY, OCTOBER 9, 1871.

THE GREAT CALAMITY OF THE AGE!

Chicago in Ashes!!

Hundreds of Millions of Dollars' Worth of Property Destroyed.

The South, the North and a Portion of the West Divisions of the City in Ruins.

All the Hotels, Banks, Public Buildings, Newspaper Offices and Great Business Blocks Swept Away.

The Conflagration Still in Progress.

Fury of the Flames.

Details, Etc., Etc.

Chicago is burning! Up to this hour of writing (1 o'clock p. m) the best part of the city is already in ashes! An area of between six and seven miles in length and nearly a mile in width, embracing the great business part of the city, has been burned over and now lies a mass of smouldering ruins!

All the principal hotels, all the public buildings, all the banks, all the newspaper offices, all the places of amusement, nearly all the great business edifices, nearly all the railroad depots, the water works, the gas works, several churches, and thousands of private residences and stores have been consumed. The proud, noble magnificent Chicago of yesterday, is to-day a mere shadow of what it was; and, helpless before the still sweeping flames, the fear is that the entire city will be consumed before we shall see the end.

The entire South Division, from Harrison street north to the river, almost the entire North Division, from the river to Lincoln Park, and several blocks in the West Division are burned.

It is utterly impossible to estimate the losses. They must in the aggregate amount to hundreds of millions of dollars. Amid the confusion and general bewilderment, we can only give a few details.

The fire broke out on the corner of DeKoven and Twelfth streets, at about 9 o'clock on Sunday evening, being caused by a cow kicking over a lamp in a stable in which a woman was milking. An alarm was immediately given, but, owing to the high southwest wind, the building was speedily consumed, and thence the fire spread rapidly. The firemen could not, with all their efforts, get the mastery of he flames. Building after building was fired by the flying cinders, which, landing on the roofs, which were as dry as tinder, owing to the protracted dry weather, instantly took fire. Northwardly and northeastwardly the flames took their course, lapping up house after house, block after block, street after street, all night long.

The scene of ruin and devastation is beyond the power of words to describe. Never, in the history of the world, has such a scene of extended, terrible and complete destruction, by conflagration, been recorded; and never has a more frightful scene of panic, distress and horror been witnessed among a helpless, sorrowing, suffering population.

It is utterly impossible, at he first thought, for he mind to take in any conception of he fearful ravages of the fire-fiend, al hough the as ounding facts stated above, is enough to appal the most heroic. The awful ru h of the si ua ion will be more fully comprehended by a glance at he following very imperfec lis of he ci y's loss. It is, however, proper to state that, at his writing, the confusion in the police and fire departments is so complete as to render it impossible to give anything like a detailed accoun of he terrible conflagra ion.

PARTIAL DETAILS OF THE LOSSES.

The first to be mentioned, and possibly the most startling feature of this carnival of flame, is the total destruction of the City Water Works, by which calamity the firemen are rendered helpless to make the least endeavor to arrest the onward march of the devouring element. Should any other fires occur in parts of the city not burning, they most certainly have their way. At about 12 o'clock last night the sheet of flames licked across the river in the neighborhood of Jackson street, first igniting a small wooden building, which communicated the fire to the Armory, and soon to the South Side Gas Works, the immense gasometer exploding with a fearful detonation, heard all over the city. Then commenced the fearful ravages, which in a few hours laid the the entire South side in ashes, north of Harrison. The Post Office and Custom House, the Chamber of Commerce, the Court House and the rest soon went down in the ocean of fire and smoke. In brief, the following prominent buildings have perished with, in almost every case, their entire contents: the New Jerusalem Church, on Adams street, and the Catholic Church, on Desplaines street.

THE JOURNAL office, the Tribune, the Times, the Republican, the Post, the Mail, the Staats Zeitung, the Union, and many other publications.

Crosby's Opera House, McVicker's Theater, Hooley's Opera House, Dearborn Theater, and Wood's Museum.

First, Second, Third, Fourth, Fifth, Union Northwestern, Manufacturers' Cook County, and Illinois National Banks.

The Second Presbyterian Church, St. Paul's Universalist Church, Trinity (Episcopal) Church.

The magnificent depot of the Chicago, Rock Island and Pacific and Lake Shore and Michigan Southern Railroads, on Van Buren street, at the head of La Salle street. The Great Central Union depot, and the Wells street depots of the Chicago and Northwestern Railroad.

The National Elevator, corner of Adams and the river, Armour, Dole & Co's Elevator, corner Market and the river, Hiram Wheeler's Elevator, on same corner as the above, the Galena Elevator, corner Rush street bridge and river, and "A" of the Illinois Central, near the Illinois Depot at the basin.

Tremont House, Sherman House, Briggs House, Metropolitan, Palmer, Adams, Bigelow, European, (Burks), Garden City and the new Pacific, in process of erection, on Clark rnd La Salle streets.

The following prominent business houses are in ashes: Field, Leitner and Co. J. V. Farwell's block, and all the magnificent blocks in that locality. The Lake Side Publishing Company's new building, on Clark street, Terrace Row, on Michigan Av. and adjacent residences.

Farwell Hall burned at about four o'clock this morning.

The great breweries, on the North Side, are gone.

In fact, as stated above, the entire South and North sides, from Harrison street, northwardly, with a few isolated buildings left standing in some remarkable manner, are in hopeless ruins,

HELP COMING.

During the night, telegrams were sent to St. Louis, Cleveland, Milwaukee and nearer cities for aid, and at the time of going to press several trains are on the way to the city, bringing free engines and men to assist us in this dire calamity.

BOARD OF TRADE.

The Board of Trade has leased for present us the northwest cor. of Washington and Canal streets We call attention to the card announcing a meeting of the Directors of the Chicago Board of Trade, to-morrow morning, at 10 o'clock, at 51 and 53 Canal Street.

COUNCIL MEETING—A PROCLAMATION.

The Common Council and a number of prominent citizens are holding a meeting this afternoon in the First Congregational Church, to make such arrangements as may be possible for the safety of the city.

The Mayor has issued a proclamation that all fires in stoves in the city shall be extinguished-

THE EVENING JOURNAL.

We are under great obligations to the Interior Printing Company, 15 and 18 Canal street, for accommodations by which we are enabled to issue this Extra. We hope before many days, to be able to announce permanent arrangements for issuing THE EVENING JOURNAL regularly. We have saved a portion of our subscription books, and hope to be able to resume publication without great delay.

The Chicago BOARD OF TRADE HAVE THEIR ROOMS AT 51 and 53 CANAL ST.

There will be a Meeting of the Directors of the Chicago

BOARD OF TRADE

AT

51 and 53 Canal St.

To-morrow, 10th, at 10 o'clock.

J. W. PRESTON, President.

This *Evening Journal* extra was printed on the premises of the Interior Printing Company in the West Division on Monday. Its account of the fire begins:

"Chicago is burning! Up to this hour of writing (1 o'clock P.M.) the best part of the city is already in ashes! An area of between six and seven miles in length, and nearly a mile in width, embracing the great business part of the city, has been burned over and now lies a mass of smoldering ruins!

"All the principal hotels, all the public buildings, all the banks, all the newspaper offices, all the places of amusement, nearly all the great business offices, nearly all the railroad depots, the water works, the gas works, several churches, and thousands of private residences and stores have been consumed. The proud, noble magnificent Chicago of yesterday is to-day a mere shadow of what it was; and, helpless before the still sweeping flames, the fear is that the entire city will be consumed before we shall see the end."

Kogan-Wendt Collection

Chicago Historical Society

Mayor Roswell B. Mason, who did his best for the city during its fiery hours, was a civil engineer, born in Oneida County, New York, in 1805. He worked his way up from teamster on the Erie Canal, at the age of seventeen, to superintendent of the Pennsylvania Canal and later of the Housatonic, New York and New Haven and the Vermont Valley railroads. He came to the Midwest in 1851 to direct the construction of the Illinois Central Railroad, a five-year job, and spent four years constructing roads in Iowa and Wisconsin before returning to railroading as superintendent of the Chicago and Alton. He was elected mayor of Chicago in 1869, and the *Historical Encyclopedia of Illinois* states that the Great Fire "tested his executive ability to the utmost."

These two proclamations by Mayor Mason are self-explanatory. Both were issued the afternoon of Monday, October 9, while the fire still burned. Many Chicagoans, however, needed no proclamation to make them behave as conscientious persons should. As soon as the newspapers resumed printing they began carrying advertisements such as these:

"Mr. McLogan, 288 Laflin, has a boy 2 or 3 years old—speaks French."

"Will the gentleman who gave me the clock and picture on State st. Oct. 9 call at 258 Cottage Grove-av. Dr. Steere."

And there was this announcement, with implications enough to supply the plot of a novel:

"PERSONAL-INFORMATION WANTED OF George Norman Beresford, who was in Chicago at the time of the fire. If this meets his eye, he is earnestly requested to communicate with his friends, who are in deep anxiety. . . . If he is in want of funds, or wishes to return home, money has been placed to his credit with E. M. Archibald, British Consul, New York. Anyone who can give information would confer a favor by addressing Claudius De La Poer Beresford, Ravencliffe, Lancashire, England."

Chicago Historical Society

An official notice, posted in the ruins on Tuesday morning, announced that the headquarters of the General Relief Committee and the temporary offices of the city government would be in the First Congregational Church at Washington and Ann streets on the near West Side. Various citizens toured the prairies to the west in horse and buggy, directing refugees to go to the church for clothing and food. Other proclamations issued by Mayor Mason at the same time were cautiously soothing, one of them ending with the words: "It is believed the fire has spent its force and all will soon be well."

Chicago Public Library

Thieves & Burglars

OFFICE OF

Pinkerton's Police.

Orders are hereby given to the Captains, Lieutenants, Sergeants and Men of Pinkerton's Preventive Police that they are in charge of the Burned District, from Polk Street, from the River to the Lake and to the Chicago River. Any person Stealing or seeking to steal any of the property in my charge, or attempt to break open the Safes, as the men cannot make arrests at the present time, they shall

Kill the Persons by my orders, no Mercy Shall be shown them, but Death shall be their fate.

Allan Pinkerton.

Chicago Historical Society

Mayor Mason was not the only one issuing proclamations, as this bloodthirsty pronouncement from Allan Pinkerton indicates. Fortunately, so far as is known, no one had to be executed by Pinkerton's officers and men.

As the fire moved on and left various areas destitute while still attacking other neighborhoods, relief stations were quickly established. Here a church pastor and his assistants are handing out food to the hungry as an armed guard stands by to prevent trouble. O. W. Clapp, a commission merchant, was appointed by Mayor Mason to supervise food distribution as the fire languished and burned itself out by the late morning of October 10. By dusk of that Tuesday, fifty carloads of food came in from nearby cities and Clapp recruited twenty volunteers from among refugees gathered at the Plymouth Church on Wabash Avenue, a place much like the one pictured here, to serve as food distributors. By late evening ten carloads of food had been given out. Only one complaint was recorded: It came from the pastor of a high-toned church, who asked Clapp if he could obtain food of better quality because of his "high-class parishioners."

A soup kitchen on Peoria Street. The server is ladling soup from a huge container, and at least one hungry customer is eating his on the spot. Because of profiteering attempts, the Common Council on Tuesday fixed the price of bread at 8 cents per 12-ounce loaf, although the city's surviving bakeries soon were turning out 10,000 to 20,000 loaves daily. The fast-buck merchants did not confine their efforts to foodstuffs. Hotel accommodations were of course in short supply, and even tiny rooms brought up to $8 a day, while a small house, which before the fire would have rented for $12 a month, now cost $75.

Some greedy landlords ousted tenants in favor of higher-paying ones, but there were compassionate citizens, too. A West Side grocer, Pat O'Connell, posted a sign reading, "All Parties Without Money Can Have Meat Here," and W. K. Nixon, in the South Division, cut rents in his newly completed building 10 percent.

A Burning Coal Pile on the North branch —

Chicago Historical Society

Another Waud drawing, using light from a burning coal pile on the river's North Branch to illuminate the shipping.

Waud's impressionistic sketch, labeled "Burning Coal," hints at the jagged ruins in the distance. The burning coal piles all over the area covered by the flames were the last vestiges of the tragedy. By early morning on October 10 hundreds of such small fires still smoldered in basements and coalyards. And by this time the fire was out. The last house in the city to be assailed by flames was that of John A. Huck, near Lake Michigan on the north side of Fullerton Avenue, then the city's northern limits.

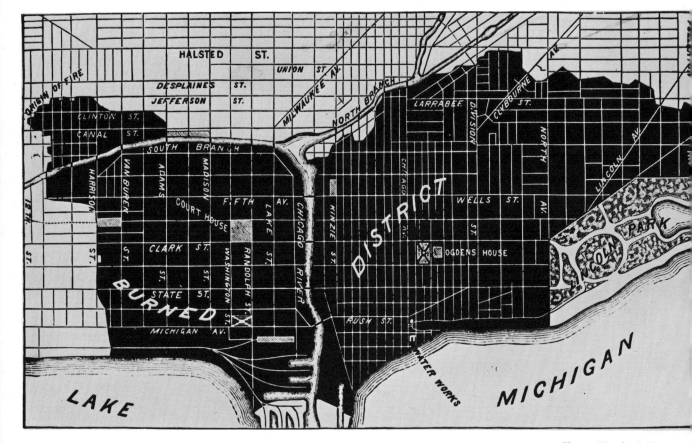

Kogan-Wendt Collection

A map showing the burned-out district with such remaining landmarks in the devastated area designated as the ruins of the Courthouse, the Water Tower and the residence of Mahlon Ogden, a civic leader, which occupied a full block in the North Division around which flames and wind swirled and which came out unscathed.

"Ruins! Ruins! Far and wide . . ."

Panoramic view of the ruins left in the wake of the Great Chicago Fire, which raged for approximately twenty-nine hours, during which $192,000,000 worth of property was wiped out. Only 120 bodies were recovered after the fire, although estimates of the dead ran as high as 300. Seventy-three miles of streets were swept by the flames, which destroyed 17,500 buildings and made 100,000 Chicagoans homeless. Other residents of the Garden City were hospitalized with injuries, and a few killed themselves because of financial losses. Millionaires became paupers overnight, and at least fifty-six insurance companies in ten states went bankrupt as a result of claims against them. A macabre coincidence, still not widely known a century later, is that on October 9, the day after the Chicago holocaust began, a river of fire roared out of the woods near the lumber town of Peshtigo, Wisconsin, and killed 1,152 persons, one of the greatest tolls ever recorded except in a war zone.

This view looks north and west from Congress Street and Wabash Avenue, not far from the Michigan Avenue Hotel, the finest bargain ever obtained by John B. Drake, owner of the Tremont House. Wandering unhappily along the lakefront just after watching the destruction of the Tremont, Drake entered the hotel and asked the owner if he would sell. The latter, believing his establishment doomed because of onrushing flames, told Drake he was crazy but took the proffered $1,000 and a promise of full payment in two weeks. As Drake left the hotel, Terrace Row, a block north, was ablaze, but swift work by firemen and the blowing up of nearby structures halted the flames before they reached the hotel. The owner tried to cancel the deal, but Drake took over the place and renamed it the Tremont.

114

Scenes along the river, sketched by Waud on the day after the end of the Great Fire, with refugees—or the curious—looking across the water at still-smoking ruins. Succinctly descriptive of this and innumerable other sights was the opening line of "From the Ruins Our City Shall Rise!": "Ruins! Ruins! Far and wide from the river and lake to the prairie side." The song was one of the first of several composed in the postfire days by George Frederick Root, the city's and the nation's leading popular composer, whose earlier works included "Tramp, Tramp, Tramp," "Battle Cry of Freedom" and "Marching Through Georgia."

One of several Gross Cyclorama panels depicting an area in the West Division ravaged by flames. Virtually all the portion of this division where the fire began was demolished, the fire's heat so intense that steel beams melted, stone flaked,

and marble was reduced to powder. A few scattered buildings in the West Division survived, including a flour mill, the Pittsburgh, Fort Wayne and Chicago Railroad depot —and, interestingly, the O'Leary house.

117

This extremely rare picture indicates, according to notations by its unknown photographer, that it is a view north from the Great Fire's point of origin on De Koven Street. If this is so, then the debris in the foreground is all that remains of the O'Leary barn, although at the time the fire started moving from it toward the north and west on that fateful Sunday night, the west wall was still standing. For weeks after the fire, sightseers came to the site of the O'Leary barn, and the newspapers, of course, carried long accounts of inquiries into the causes. A measure of the disregard for accuracy on the part of many of the journals may be had by comparing two descriptions of Mrs. O'Leary carried by a single newspaper, despotic and irascible Wilbur Fisk Storey's *Times*. On October 18 she was "an old hag . . . whose very appearance indicated great poverty. She apparently was about seventy years of age and was bent almost double with the weight of many years of toil, and trouble, and privation." In the December 3 *Times*' story of the inquiry, she was described this way: "She is a tall, stout, Irish woman with no intelligence. . . . During her testimony, the infant she held . . . kicked its bare legs around and drew nourishment from mammoth reservoirs."

The Lake Shore and Michigan Southern Railroad depot before and after. Work on this depot, designed by William W. Boyington, began in 1866. It was to accommodate the Michigan Southern and the Chicago, Rock Island and Pacific and was located between Jackson and Van Buren streets and Sherman and Griswold streets. The three-story structure, made of Joliet limestone, was completed in the spring of 1867 at a cost of $225,000.

This was how Lake Street looked after the fire, if you gazed eastward along it from State Street toward the lake. One of the numerous deaths occurred on Lake Street at the river, where a hurrying man, with an armload of clothing, stumbled and fell into the water through the opening in a broken railing. No one tried to rescue him.

Chicago Fire Department

Lake Street, looking eastward from Clark Street, a block above the Courthouse. Although this "Street of Merchants" had started to be supplanted by State Street as the city's main business thoroughfare, a number of important business houses still remained. Among them was a store owned by Elias R. Bowen, who sold military and lodge uniforms. It was Bowen who "rescued" the Long John's horses and finally found a safe refuge for them. But he arrived at his own establishment too late to save anything but a few maps, books and papers. His uninsured loss totaled about $15,000. Lake Street was a favorite spot for looters during the fire. One, removing goods from J. B. Shay and Company's building despite the shouted protests of employees, was about to leave with a store trunk laden with loot when a clerk drew a revolver and threatened to use it.

"Fire and be damned!" cried the thief.

The clerk put the gun away.

Chicago Fire Department

The ornate front wall is virtually all that was left of the Farwell Building on Washington Street, whose arched doorway frames an open safe from which someone has removed whatever valuables survived. The printed handbill, just to the right of the steps, is proof how important even the most trivial things can become in an emergency. It is an advertisement announcing the availability of lead pencils.

Chicago Fire Department

East on Monroe Street from Clark Street, two blocks below the Courthouse. Attorney George Payson, whose offices were on Clark Street a block north of this corner, has left a fine description of what it was like there at 2 A.M. Monday:

"A few persons . . . came and went like specters. They either had nothing to tell, or no time to tell it in. The wind was bewildering, for it seemed to come from every quarter and with a fury I had hardly ever seen before. Showers of sparks rained all around me and blew along the pavements, threatening to start a fresh fire at every turn."

Payson saw no firemen, no equipment, almost no passersby. His reaction: "The great city was left to burn alone, without any attempt to save it."

A portion of the battered Courthouse still stands, but little else remains in this vista east on Randolph
Street. This photograph may have
been taken from the roof of the
Lind Block, the only building undamaged in the business section.

Chicago *Sun-Times*

126

Testimony to the accuracy of the *Tribune*'s report is this block on Washington Street facing the Courthouse. It described the aftermath as "more widespread, soul-sickening desolation than mortal eye ever beheld since the destruction of Jerusalem. The proud and stately city of yesterday for miles around had sunk into cellars and basements. What had hours before been the mart of commerce was now an indescribable chaos of broken columns, fallen walls, streets covered with debris, melted metal, charred and blackened trees standing up like spectres. The tall spires of churches, the Courthouse dome, the stately blocks that were the pride of the city and the admiration of visitors, the noted landmarks . . . everything had disappeared."

The Courthouse as it appeared before the fire and afterward, with the trees gone and the cupola fallen in. The views are not identical for distance and angle, but there is a reason. The building from which the first photograph was taken probably is represented by the foreground ruins in the second shot. One of the freak escapes from death was recorded near the Courthouse, where a huge St. Bernard dog, whose nightly duty was to remain in the fireproof vaults of the Fidelity Safe Deposit Insurance Company, next door to the Sherman House, was found unharmed when the vaults were opened.

West entrance to the Courthouse on La Salle Street. The gentleman in the top hat seems to be reading one of the numerous placards on the building. The larger poster to his left tells of the work of the Chicago Relief and Aid Society.

View southeast from the Courthouse, with wagons standing by to remove debris. This photograph was taken on Tuesday morning, when essential services were being partially restored. As soon as nearby telegraph offices reopened, Chicagoans thronged there to inform relatives and friends in other cities of their fates. One businessman sent this classic wire to his wife, who was visiting in New York: "STORE AND CONTENTS, DWELLING AND EVERYTHING LOST. INSURANCE WORTHLESS. SEE SMITH IMMEDIATELY. TELL HIM TO BUY ALL THE COFFEE HE CAN AND SHIP THIS AFTERNOON BY EXPRESS. DON'T CRY."

Chicago Historical Society

Looking north from the Courthouse, across the rubble that once was the Sherman House and up Clark Street. The square of canvas in the lower foreground, just next to the horsecar tracks, seems to be a cover for a peddler's wagon. Several customers are discernible, waiting their turn to buy whatever is being sold.

The view is northwest from the Courthouse. The fire
has been over for several days, and the small frame
building almost at the center of this photograph carries
the legend "Bauer and Loenitz, Architects."

Rubble, rubble everywhere, looking east from the Courthouse. Somewhere in the ashes and ruins of Randolph Street from Clark to State streets are poker chips, roulette tables and other effects of establishments along Hairtrigger Block, which boasted some of the most elaborate gambling places in the country, most notably the Senate and Ted Cameron's house, which gave all patrons free duck dinners and wine.

This drawing of a youngster standing or sitting in the Courthouse bell, as it lay in the basement after the fire, may have more significance when one learns that the huge bell was a target for souvenir hunters. Some of the metal from it was fash-ioned into rings and scarf pins even before the 7,200 pounds that re-mained were sold at auction for 62½ cents a pound to Thomas Bryan, who announced he would melt it—to make rings and scarf pins.

Chicago Fire Department

Did the ladder into this open window of the First National Bank at State and Washington streets provide access for an officer of the bank checking up on the contents or for an opportunistic thief with the same idea in mind? It's anyone's guess. The damage to the building was estimated at $160,000, but A. T. Andreas, in his mammoth three-volume *History of Chicago* (1885) says of the First National: "The great fire partially destroyed the bank building, and after a temporary removal, on January 1, 1872, the management occupied their rebuilt structure, corner of Washington and State streets. The safes and vaults of the building had been quite unharmed; not a security or valuable was lost, and the business . . . proceeded uninterruptedly after the week of the fire."

Chicago Fire Department

The Merchants' Loan and Trust Company building at Dearborn and Lake streets did not fare nearly so well as the First National Bank.

Waud came across some men searching the ruins of
a business establishment for the safe, hidden by fallen
debris. This is his quick sketch.

searching ruins for a Safe

Chicago Public Library

Chicago Public Library

The recovery of safes from the ruins of various business places was difficult but vital. Sometimes when safes were opened too early, the overheated contents burst into flames as soon as the air hit them. Consequently, as seen above, water was poured onto the safes until the metal was chilled all the way through. Even with safety measures, results were unpredictable. In most large safes, when they were successfully opened, valuables were whole, but before this fact could be ascertained, some of the local bankers considered paying off depositors at the rate of 25 cents on the dollar. Chauncey Blair, president of the Merchants' National Bank, put a stop to that. "If a dollar is found in the vaults of the Merchants' National Bank when they are reached and opened," he intoned, "that dollar belongs to the depositors!" The rest of the bankers fell into line.

Rubble and ruin on a stretch of Clark Street. Nearby, at Randolph and Dearborn streets, what the newspapers called Thieves' Corner was now a smoldering memory, but in its heyday it had been the center of an area the *Journal* decried as "so contaminated by execrable vagabonds that respectable persons avoid it as they would a cesspool."

The Sherman House, before and after the arrival of its most boisterous guest. In the early hours of the Great Fire, even while flames licked at the Courthouse across the street, hundreds of patrons gathered on the immense flat roof of the hotel to extinguish brands that rained down upon them. Suddenly, many fiery tongues of flame burst out of scores of windows, and there was a mass exodus from the roof to the street. So rapid was the spread of the blaze through the building that a few people were trapped, and many others escaped with the greatest difficulty. The hotel's proprietors, within hours after the building went down in ruins, rented quarters at Canal and Madison streets and made plans for a new Sherman House, which was duly constructed and became, as in the past, a gathering place for celebrities, politicians and world-famed travelers.

No one ever checked into the Grand Pacific Hotel, which occupied the entire block bounded by Clark, La Salle, Jackson and Quincy streets. The hotel, which was being built with $600,000 raised through the sale of stock, was made of Ohio sandstone and would have been the city's finest. It had 100 private parlors, each with bath, and 450 single rooms; the upper floors were served by steam-propelled "vertical railways," which moved "as lightly and as smoothly as a cloud rises in the summer air." Tanks below the roof had a capacity of 12,000 gallons of water which could be emptied into any part of the building on short notice. Unfortunately, these tanks had not yet been filled when the fire came. Moreover, its upper floors were too high for the stream thrown by the Long John to reach them against the wind.

143

A closer look at the Grand Pacific, showing how complete the destruction was. Somewhere in that jumble of fallen stone is the carriage court, once covered with a glass dome, in which a dozen omnibuses at once would have been able to discharge or pick up passengers.

Chicago Public Library

144

The La Salle Street entrance to the Grand Pacific, so modern a hostelry that its basement held a laundry and a bakery. When stones from the blazing upper stories began hurtling down into the street, endangering the lives of the firemen, a Fire Department official came by and ordered the Long John to move on. As the foreman uncoupled the hose, a falling block of stone hit the boiler, cutting away a bolt and three rivets. Then the firemen, unable to find the Long John's horses, trundled the fire engine out of harm's way by hand.

Doorway to the Masonic Temple on Dearborn Street, near Washington. The notice on whatever lies in the street in the foreground reads: "SHOW CASES! SHOW CASES! 13 N. Green St. S. P. Martin."

Interestingly, there was another new hotel besides the Grand Pacific that never got to open its doors for patrons. The Bigelow House, adjoining the mammoth Honore Block at Adams and Dearborn streets, stood four stories high and had been built by Captain George A. Bigelow at a cost of $225,000 and furnished by him for an additional $200,000. It was to receive its first guests on the morning of October 9; but no one ever signed the register, and few glimpsed the welcoming roses on the black walnut tables in the dining room as the building turned into ashes and debris.

Kogan-Wendt Collection

The Honore Block was as completely destroyed as the neighboring Bigelow House. Its end was spectacular, with the three top stories, twisted out of shape by the inferno, crashing down into Adams Street. These two photographs graphically illustrate the extent of the fire's damage to the office building, with the one above also furnishing a view of the remains of the Post Office Building farther north on Dearborn Street.

Chicago *Sun-Times*

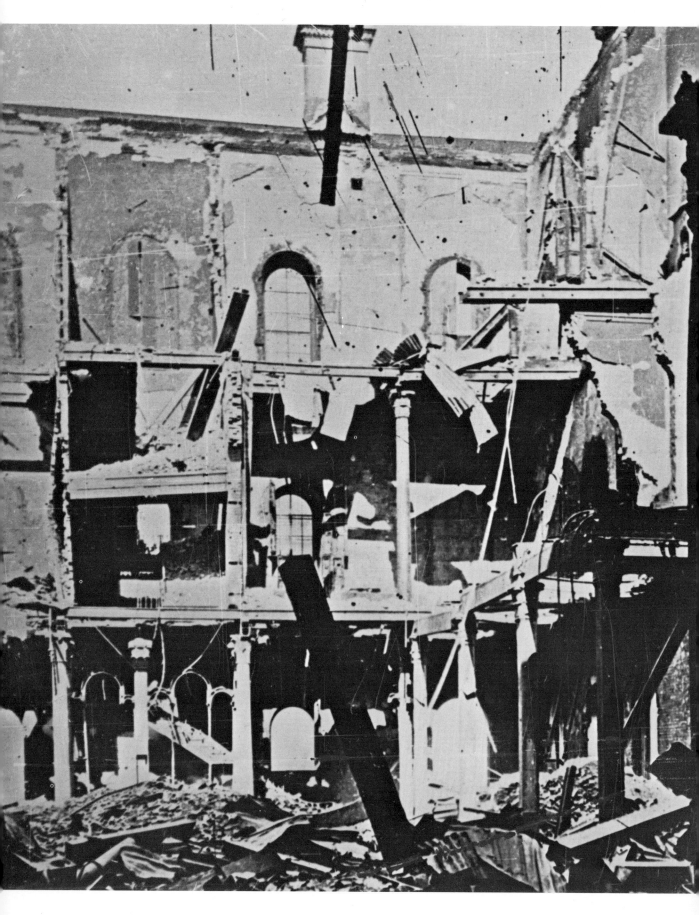

Chicago Fire Department

The Post Office and Customs House Building, in the midst of whose ruins searchers found the Post Office cat, soaked but safe, in half a bucket of water, to which she had wisely retreated.

One of the heroes of the Great Fire was Alonzo Hannis, a postal clerk, who found his way to the Post Office district as the Courthouse was burning and joined the night watchman and the night superintendent of mails, David Green. Hannis asked permission to begin packing the mail for removal and was threatened with discharge by Green "if you touch any letters without orders from headquarters." Green then left to look at the fire, and Hannis began tossing the mail into sacks. Green returned and this time said nothing.

Eventually other employees showed up, and most of the mail was indeed saved. But Hannis continued working until 4:30 A.M., when the building was ordered cleared, using the light from the burning Lombard and Reynolds buildings nearby for illumination. As he left, he found an overlooked sack of first class mail and took it to the lakefront. There he left the pouch with a woman seated near a pile of household goods. Asked whether she would keep an eye on the mail while he found a wagon, she arose, spread her dress over the bag, and seated herself once more, telling Hannis: "If anyone attempts to take the mail, I will shoot him on the spot."

Before-and-after views of the Post Office and Customs House. Ironically, this building was highly touted when it went up in 1855 as Chicago's first "completely fireproof structure" because of the use of heavy walls and wrought-iron beams. Experts claimed that it was almost completely destroyed in the Great Fire because the beams had not been fully encased in the masonry. After the blaze, the walls that remained standing were used as part of a building housing Haverly's Theater until the site at Dearborn and Monroe streets was taken over in 1881 for the new First National Bank.

Another view of the Post Office which shows how the interior walls and floors collapsed. The Post Office vaults were opened on the Saturday after the fire with a Treasury Department man and a detail of troops on hand. It was discovered that the vaults had sustained injury in their plunge into the basement, and of the currency which had been in an iron-lined vault, only portions of $19,000 worth of gold certificates were discovered, of which $16,500 were redeemable. Another $37,000 in currency was found untouched in a different safe, but the total loss in currency and coin certificates was $1,034,300 for which the Collector of the Port, James E. McLean, was legally responsible. Congress, however, passed special legislation to exempt him from having to come up with the money.

The Field and Leiter store before and after the fire
Marshall Field and Levi Z. Leiter showed up early
long before the flames actually threatened, and Harlow
Higinbotham, young head of their accounting and
insurance department, ordered wagons from the com
pany barns to wait in readiness behind the store. Mean
while, a fire was started in the furnace so there would
be steam for the elevators, and workers began firs
removing the finest goods, which were taken to th
lakeshore nearby and unloaded as the wagons re
turned for more salvage. At last, after the gas ha
failed and work was continuing by candlelight, Field
took a squad of men to the roof to fight the sparks, a
wet blankets were hung over the windows to protect th
glass. But the battle was lost when blazing wood bega
hitting the roof. The windows cracked, and other flam
ing debris came inside the building.

Eventually the store was abandoned, and the wagon
returned to the lakeshore, where much of the store
inventory was under guard, to take some $600,00
worth of goods to the South Side to be stored in Leiter
home, the carbarns and an obliging church. One enter
prising clerk saved $20,000 worth of silks and lace b
driving it out of the area on a horsecar.

When the building walls finally fell, a tailor, Samue
Shawcross, who was hurrying through the alley to h
Washington Street store, was trapped under them.

154

All that was left of the Marble Palace and some $2,500,000 worth of stock and furnishings which Field and Leiter were unable to save. The two must have found money somewhere, however, for the sign on the post reads: "Cash boys and girls will be paid what is due them Monday 9 A.M. Oct. 16th at 60 Calumet Ave. Field, Leiter, & Co." Ultimately, the firm became Marshall Field and Company, with a world-famous spacious State Street store between Washington and Randolph streets.

The *Tribune* Building, as it was and as it became. A stone structure described as "absolutely fireproof," it stood at the southeast corner of Dearborn and Madison streets. It had been built in 1869 at a cost of $250,000. It appeared for a while that the fire would pass the building, but 3 A.M. Monday Joseph Medill, its editor, became worried and took a team of men to the roof, which was covered with a "fireproof" material which—Medill had noted—seemed to grow soft in direct sunlight. Soon fifteen or twenty men, with buckets, shovels and boards, were beating out sparks and soaking the roof, which did indeed catch fire several times. Meanwhile, offices on the west side of the building grew so hot that the window glass cracked and varnish on the furniture began to smoke. At about 7 A.M. the situation was so perilous that Medill ordered the building evacuated. Those who had been on the roof searched the offices as they left, finding several employees asleep from exhaustion.

Conrad Kahler, a *Tribune* pressman, bumped into John McDevitt, former billiards champion, as he left the doomed building. McDevitt was heading up the alley toward Tom Foley's billiard parlor on Dearborn Street. Kahler grabbed him by the arm to warn him, but the other shook him loose, saying, "Oh, the hell with you." He died in the flames.

Kahler then discovered a drunken stranger asleep on the steps leading to the basement entrance of the *Tribune* and received a similar rebuff when he shook him awake to warn him that death was near unless he moved immediately. "That's none of your damned business," the stranger growled. His fate was never learned.

Chicago *Tribune*

156

Booksellers' Row, with its ghost. It is part of Great Fire lore and legend that after the fire nothing legible remained from the million or more volumes stacked in the various shops but a single page from the Bible. This contained a portion of the Lamentations of Jeremiah: "How doth the city sit solitary, that was full of people! how is she become a widow! she that was great among the nations. . . . She weepeth sore in the night, and her tears are on her cheeks."

Chicago Fire Department

Crosby's Opera House again, with its new decorations not even given time enough to become a memory. Next door at the St. James Hotel a distraught husband hired a hack driver to remove his invalid wife from danger, offering $60. Before the passengers were aboard a jeweler, not knowing the vehicle was engaged, dashed up to promise the driver $500 to save his stock. The greedy hackman slammed the door and started to pull away when two men yanked him from his seat and helped the sick woman and her husband inside. A third bystander then drove the couple to safety.

It would take more than a lottery to save Crosby's this time, as a completely unscheduled performance brought down the house.

The Second Presbyterian Church, at the corner of Wabash Avenue and Washington Street, was known as one of the finest in the West. It was built with bituminous limestone, which exuded crude petroleum, and the mottled stone gave rise to two nicknames: the Spotted Church and, for the less reverent, the Church of the Holy Zebra. The church cost $45,000 to erect and was valued at about $55,000. Because of the encroachment of business, it had been decided on October 1 to move farther south and merge with the Olivet Presbyterian, which was at Wabash Avenue and Fourteenth Street. The first services of the combined congregations had been held on Sunday, October 8, at Olivet Presbyterian..

Chicago *Sun-Times*

Michigan Avenue, north from Madison Street. This was not far from the Chicago Club, at 168 Michigan Avenue, which provided an elegant morsel for the flames. Several of the club members, whose homes or businesses had been burned out overnight, gathered at the club for breakfast Monday morning, only to be driven out when that building also caught fire. But the clubmen retreated in good order, taking with them a sofa, a bottle of whiskey and some cigars, so they could top off their late-morning meal comfortably on the lakeshore.

Neither the policeman nor the two men inspecting these ruins seem very interested, and if you didn't know this was Wells and South Water streets, you might well imagine you were looking at a junkyard. Laborers working in the business district did so at grave peril to themselves. Three were killed on South Water Street when a wall fell, and more were crushed to death under other collapsing structures.

Chicago Fire Department

Only the main part of the Chicago River seems usable in this view eastward to Lake Michigan from Michigan Avenue. Elsewhere, the two branches of the river were mostly clogged with masses of charred wood, skeletons of fallen bridges and hulks of vessels. Of a scene in the North Branch of the river, an anonymous citizen—and obviously a poetically inclined one—was quoted by Everett Chamberlain and Elias Colbert in their book *The Great Conflagration* as saying: "One or two propellers were hugging the hither shore, like white doves frightened from their nests, and shrinking toward what semblance of cover offered itself, if, perchance, it might shelter them from the fell pursuer."

Chicago *Tribune*

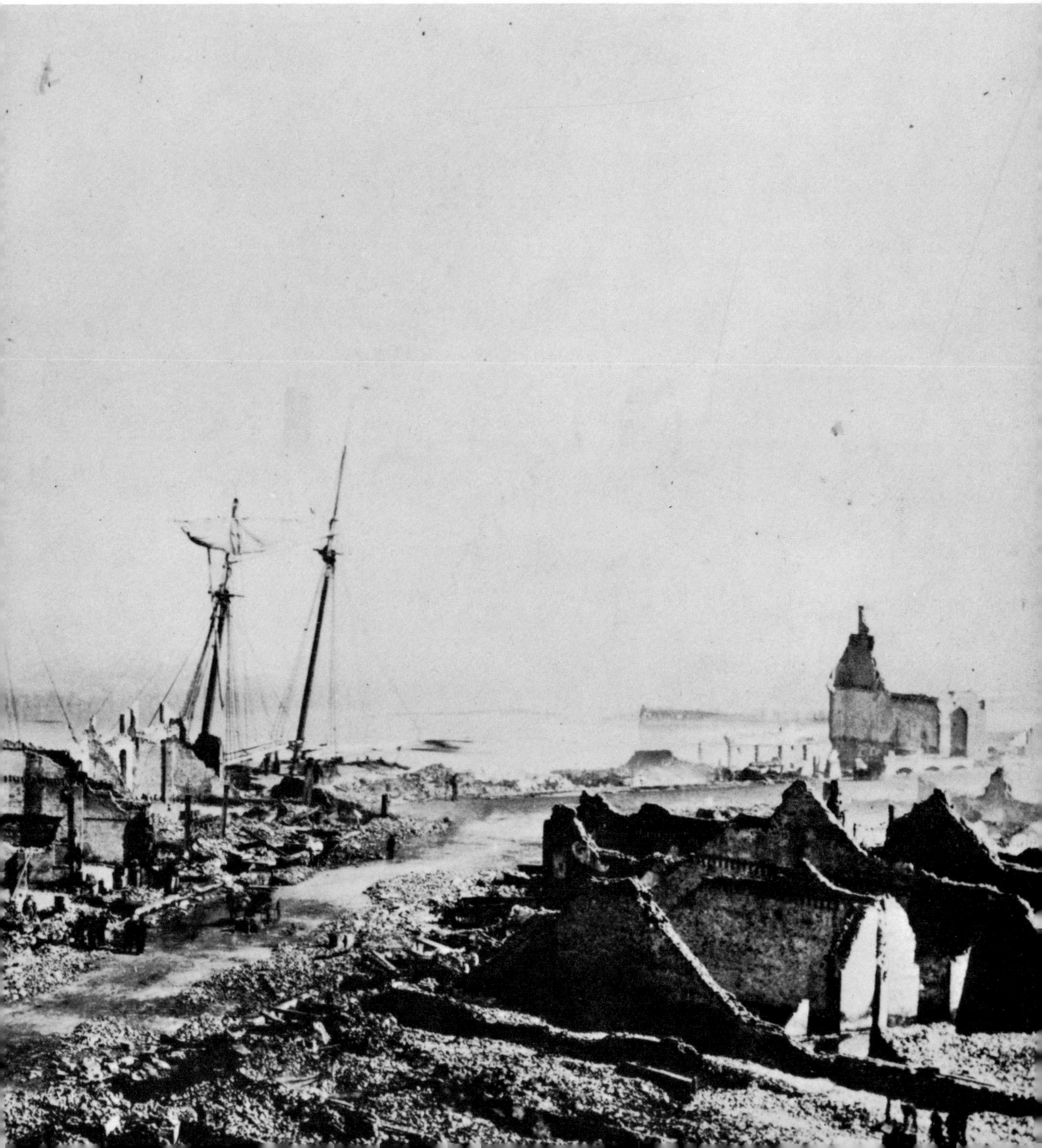

The remains of the Rush Street Bridge leading to the North Division. What happened to the bridgetender—or why and when he fled—is not known. But the river shipping, with fire running up the rigging of many vessels and turning some masts into giant candles, along with the squat bridges with superstructures aflame, added a grotesque touch to the awesome spectacle.

Chicago *Tribune*

Looking north across the river at Franklin Street, where Olcott's Coal Yard, visible behind the cluster of masts, seems to have escaped unscathed. This was not far from the Madison Street Bridge, which was in grave danger as flames raced greedily up the river's east bank. But Andrew Boyer, the sixty-year-old bridgetender there, refused to flee. Instead, he swung the center-mounted revolving span parallel to the banks—as he would have done in a more tranquil time to make space for a ship to pass—whenever the flames drew near. To all who cried out to him to flee, he replied: "I will save my bridge!" Meanwhile, Boyer's two sons anxiously waited below the bridge in a small boat, ready to fish him out of the water if the flames or heat forced him to jump. The boys did rescue several strangers who were driven into the river. Boyer's skillful manipulation of the bridge worked, for he did save it.

Rush Medical College, the first such school west of Cincinnati and Lexington, Kentucky, was built in 1844, though the first classes were held in 1843 in rented rooms, with a faculty of four and a total enrollment of twenty-two. The building shown here was the school's third, erected in 1867 at a cost of $70,000.

Cromie Collection

Chicago *Daily News*

For something which had been described as "perfectly fireproof," the Chicago Historical Society building at Dearborn and Ontario streets fared poorly. When it finally became clear that the fireproof qualities—such as they were—were not enough to save the building, William Corkran, the thirty-two-year-old librarian, and an elderly janitor removed the original of the Emancipation Proclamation from its frame and took Lincoln's walking stick from its case, as well as one of George P. A. Healy's paintings hanging on the wall. But everything else was abandoned to the flames when the men were warned that the first floor was ablaze. They raced down the stairs as explosions began and the skylight dropped to the floor below. They darted through the lecture room, which was on fire, and went out the window into a garden. Corkran escaped, but the janitor perished. Losses included 150,000 pamphlets, 18,000 books, a pike which had been owned by John Brown and several of Healy's paintings.

Chicago Public Library

St. James' Episcopal Church, the first of its denomination organized in Chicago, was at Cass (now Wabash Avenue) and Illinois streets originally but moved into a new building at Cass and Huron streets in 1857. This later was enlarged and a tower was added, so that the final cost of the church at the time of the fire was almost $200,000. As is evident in the postfire photograph, the tower itself escaped virtually untouched, although the church portion was almost completely destroyed.

Chicago Public Library

Chicago *Sun-Times*

The New England Congregational Church, dedicated in 1867, stood at Dearborn and White (now Delaware Place) streets. The building was of unpolished Athens marble, and niches above the pillars at the front doorway held: (1) a piece of stone from the first Scottish church where the Congregational creed was adopted, (2) a sliver of rock from Delft Haven, where the Puritans held their last service in 1620 before embarking for the New World, and (3) a bit of Plymouth Rock. The interior woodwork was of black walnut, carved and ornamented.

Isaac Arnold, an attorney and former Congressman who had been a member of the honor guard which accompanied Lincoln's body to Illinois, lived at Erie and Pine streets and, when awakened about 1:30 A.M. Monday morning, believed his spacious yard might permit the saving of his home. Arnold, his servants and three children began doing their best to beat back whatever advance embers arrived. But soon thirteen - year - old Arthur Arnold shouted that the barn and the hay were in flames, and when this was quickly followed by fire on the roof, in the greenhouse, and on the front porch, topped off by word that the water had stopped, Arnold sounded retreat. He seized an armful of private papers, and everyone headed for the lake.

Kogan-Wendt Collection

Alma Smith Collection

The remnants of the George Rumsey mansion at Huron and Cass streets in the North Division, immediately east of the home of his brother, Julian, a former mayor. Julian Rumsey's grounds held not only a fountain stocked with brook trout, but a small building in which was installed one of the first billiard tables in town. When the fire broke out, Julian went south to his office and returned with insurance receipts valued at $60,000. Later, as he left his home for the last time, he took a painting from the wall—the first valuable one purchased by the Rumseys after their marriage—and paid a passerby $12.50 to save it. The painting later was returned unharmed.

The only building completely unscathed in the business district was the Lind Block, occupied by the Z. M. Hall Wholesale Grocery firm, at the northwest corner of Randolph and Market streets. "This was saved," wrote Elias Colbert and Everett Chamberlain in *The Great Conflagration*, "by its isolated location, being on the shore of the river, and separated by an exceptionally wide street from the seething furnace which consumed all else in the vicinity."

Chicago *Tribune*

Farther north, another surviving structure was the modest home of Patrolman Richard Bellinger, who lived on Lincoln Place (now Hudson Avenue) near Lincoln Park. The newly married Bellinger, helped by his brother-in-law, also a policeman, tore up the wooden sidewalk, the picket fence and the front steps and raked and burned all the dried leaves in his yard. Then Bellinger covered the roof of his home with wet rugs and lined up filled buckets of water at the bottom of a ladder leaning against the house. He and his brother-in-law then battled flying embers for some hours and won. This photograph was taken in 1961, and the plaque on the front of the house reads: "This Is Policeman Bellinger's Cottage, Saved by His Heroic Efforts from the Chicago Fire. October, 1871."

Most famous of the surviving structures was the home of Mahlon Ogden, seen here from two different perspectives. The three-story frame house, in which the civic leader and brother of the city's first mayor had lived with his family since it was built twelve years earlier, stood on Lafayette Place (now Walton Street) facing Washington Square in the North Division.

Ogden was awakened at about 1 A.M. on Monday. After rushing into the business district to save some of his papers from his office and trying without success to rescue his brother-in-law's house, he concentrated on salvaging his own, with the help of numerous relatives and friends who had taken refuge on the grounds.

Carpets soaked with cistern water were hung on the sides of the building. Patrols beat out the wooden fence when it caught fire. Men with buckets and brooms kept the flames from the mansard roof. When the situation appeared most critical, the wind died down long enough to ease the crisis, and when the sidewalk on adjoining Dearborn Street caught fire, the wind obligingly blew the flames away from the house.

As a precaution, Mrs. Ogden took the family silver in a lumber wagon to a place of safety, but the action was needless. The fire finally abandoned the Ogden House in favor of easier victims. Later, neighbors who had lost their homes were angered at the Ogdens' good fortune, and he and his family received threats for weeks after the Great Fire. The Newberry Library now stands on the site of the Ogden House.

Kogan-Wendt Collection

"Chicago Shall Rise Again!"

One of the proudest aspects of Chicago history is the speed with which the city recovered from the Great Fire. Rival cities, even those from which food and clothing were rushed to the hapless sufferers, considered the disaster a fatal blow to Chicago's future. A New Orleans newspaper exulted: "Chicago will never be like the Carthage of old. Its glory will be of the past, not of the present, while its hopes, once so bright and cloudless, will be to the end marred and blackened by the smoke of its fiery fate." Other editorialists, reflecting on Chicago's deserved reputation as one of the wickedest cities in the country, what with its Levee district of brothels, vice dens and saloons and its scores of gambling houses, considered the Great Fire proper retribution: "Again the fire of heaven has fallen on Sodom and Gomorrah!"

Many Chicagoans fled, never to return. Far, far more remained, both rich and poor agreeing with the sentiments expressed by the *Tribune*'s editorial headed "CHEER UP!" on the day after the last flames were out: "In the midst of a calamity without parallel in the world's history, looking upon the ashes of thirty years' accumulations, the people of this once beautiful city have resolved that CHICAGO SHALL RISE AGAIN!" The photograph on the left depicts one of hundreds of projects that sprang up, the Marine Company and adjacent buildings as they appeared when partially completed in 1872 at La Salle and Lake streets. Combined with the surge of reconstruction was the undoubted and fortuitous fact that some of the city's prime assets outside the range of the Great Fire escaped destruction—the Union Stockyards, miles of Lake Michigan docks, most of the railroad trunk lines and several hundred factories. Four years after the holocaust, Chicago bragged that it was the meat-packing center of the nation, and so complete did its recovery strike visitors that many considered it "the marvel of the age." An ebullient writer in *Lakeside Monthly* summed up the feelings of many: "This is a peerless metropolis in its indomitability of spirit, in its solidity of structure, in its imposing architecture, in its development of a sleepless vitality, an unaltering faith and an irrepressible progressive impulse."

Chicago *Daily News*

A rare photograph of the O'Leary and McLaughlin cottages on De Koven Street. Both escaped almost unscathed, although the boarded-up windows of the O'Leary place hint that some damage was caused—or that action had been taken to prevent vandalism by souvenir hunters. The tethered cow was identified in this contemporary photograph as the actual culprit responsible for kicking over the lantern in the O'Leary barn and touching off the conflagration.

Another view of the O'Leary place and adjoining cottages, which, as the site where the Great Fire was born, naturally drew throngs of curious visitors immediately afterward. The attached O'Leary and McLaughlin cottages are shown from the rear, and the timbers around which most of the crowd has clustered would seem to be all that remained of the O'Leary barn in which the blaze began.

The first entrepreneurs after the flames passed the business district were three young men who set up this establishment with an old sideboard, a barrel and some glasses with a total investment of $2.50. Schock, Bigford & Co. sold cigars, tobacco, grapes, apples and cider at this stand at 169 Dearborn Street opposite the wreckage of the Post Office.

A jerry-built shack, 12 by 16 feet, was the first actual building erected in the business area. W. D. Kerfoot, a real estate dealer, aided by his clerk and the clerk's father, put it up, as seen in the drawing at the left, on October 10 at 89 Washington Street, between Clark and Dearborn streets. His buoyant slogan, crudely lettered on a board and placed above the entrance, has rung down the years as a symbol of Chicago's resurgent spirit: "ALL GONE BUT WIFE, CHILDREN & ENERGY." This shack was up in a single morning and was called Kerfoot's Block. Nine days later, when the surroundings had cooled sufficiently, the Board of Public Works asked Kerfoot to move his building inside the sidewalk line. He not only did so, but expanded the original structure and affixed several additional signs, as seen in the photograph below.

Meanwhile, life resumed its more or less normal pace in the days immediately after the holocaust. In this contemporary drawing, a marriage ceremony is performed amid the ruins of a local church.

The Reverend Robert Collyer preached outside the still-standing walls of the Unity Church on Dearborn Street, diagonally across from Mahlon Ogden's house, on the first Sunday after the Great Fire. He told his parishioners that he had been trying all week "to reach such a spiritual height that I could look down upon all the devastation and thank God for all" and, in a typically Chicago spirit of the times, added, "We have not lost, first, our geography. Nature called the lakes, the forests, the prairies together in convention long before we were born, and they decided that on this spot a great city would be built." The Unity Church was rebuilt in 1872.

Strolling through the burned-out area on the Sunday after the holocaust, Waud sketched this scene of the Reverend R. M. Parkhurst preaching in a makeshift pulpit outside the partially demolished Grace Methodist Church. The prime contemporary Chicago historian A. T. Andreas recorded that "a considerable number of the widely separated members assembled upon the ruins of their temple and resolved to stand by the Society." Fifty-six days later, regular services were held in a temporary building on the site, and a new Grace Methodist Church went up the next year at La Salle and Locust streets.

Sketch by Theodore R. Davis in *Harper's Weekly* of hastily erected shanties on the North Side which sheltered some of the refugees. One woman cooks in this basement community, another cuddles her infant, and a man and two youngsters dig for something in the rubble.

Chicagoans had to travel long distances for water in many cases. These are shown filling buckets, and for the youngster what seems to be a teakettle, at the artesian well in Lincoln Park. Wagons carrying barrels are being loaded in the background, perhaps by enterprising merchants who peddled water through the town.

Eager young merchants did a brisk business selling souvenirs, especially items salvaged from commercial buildings, churches and theaters. Sightseers came quickly, many on special excursion trains which started running on the Sunday after the Great Fire. Among the earliest visitors was John Jex Bardwell, a Detroit photographer, who took pictures of the ruins.

Chicago Public Library

Built with materials salvaged from the Great Fire's ruins, the Relic House stood on Clark Street across from Lincoln Park for some sixty years. It was a favorite beer garden-*cum*-museum until it was torn down in the 1930's. At one time it was owned by the father of movie star Gloria Swanson.

Cromie Collection

Young ladies preparing sandwiches and distributing them to some of the city's thousands of burned-out children. Besides food, some 300 mattresses of hay, excelsior and cornhusks were made by local upholsterers for distribution by the Ladies Relief Society that was organized on October 19 in the home of a local social leader, Mrs. Wirt Dexter. A month after the fire was over, some 60,000 persons were still being cared for at various distributing points in the city.

There was a dire shortage of clothing, and in this drawing of a relief station, wearing apparel of all sorts is being distributed. One of the first directives to his teachers by School Superintendent J. L. Pickard when the schools reopened on October 23 was to check pupils' clothing and determine if those who were absent from classes had stayed away because they had nothing to wear. After this survey was made, clothing and money were distributed to needy young ones.

Chicago Public Library

189

RELIEF FOR CHICAGO

The citizens of Rockford are requested to meet at

Brown's Hall,

This Tuesday Evening, Oct. 10, '71,

AT 7 1-2 O'CLOCK, to devise means for the immediate

RELIEF OF THE DESTITUTE

Of Chicago, whose misfortunes appeal so loudly to our sympathy and benevolence. **Let Every Man Come.**

COOKED FOOD
WANTED.

A telegram from the Rockford Committee, to Mayor Bronson, received this morning, reads as follows:

"One hundred thousand people are on the open prairie, without food. Let every family that can spare a pound of meat or bread, give it at once. Send nothing but Cooked Food.'

Send contributions to Brown's Hall, day and evening.

The Rockford Committee will return from Chicago this evening, and report to the meeting to-night.

The Mayor of Chicago telegraphs this morning that people of neighboring towns are requested not to come there at present.

By Order of Relief Committee.

Aid from a multitude of cities for the survivors and sufferers was quick and plentiful. The handbill to the left is addressed to citizens of a mid-northern Illinois town, along with a concluding plea that went largely unheeded: "The Mayor of Chicago telegraphs this morning that people of neighboring towns are requested not to come here at present." Above, a contemporary drawing shows a railroad depot in New York, a scene duplicated many times in other parts of the country. From Oconomowoc, Wisconsin, the owner of the Townsend House came to Chicago to advise all former patrons and their friends of his offer of free lodgings. By October 20 Phoebe Cozzens of St. Louis had been to Chicago twice with supplies from the Ladies' Christian Society of St. Louis. Cincinnati set up a free soup kitchen on Chicago's West Side where 3,500 refugees were fed every day through December. President Grant sent a personal check for $1,000. In all, some $5,000,000 was contributed, one-fifth from twenty-nine foreign countries.

This is the lobby of a Fifth Avenue hotel in New
York, with a score of men discussing the most ex-
citing news of the day—the Great Fire in Chicago.

Chicago Public Library

THE GREAT CALAMITY.

THE BUSINESS PORTION OF CHICAGO IN ASHES!

Loss Estimated at One Hundred and Fifty Millions.

WHOLESALE DESTRUCTION OF INSURANCE COMPANIES!

THE STAUNCH OLD BULWARK,

THE INSURANCE CO. OF NORTH AMERICA!

Comes out of the terrible ordeal still Vigorous and Strong.

To Agents of the Insurance Company of North America:

GENTLEMEN :

You must be anxious to learn the fate of this Company at Chicago ; and while our losses have been immense, I am happy to say they *do not exceed one-half of the Net Surplus* of the Company, and that the venerable old Bulwark of 1794 is still strong and vigorous, and able to offer the best of security to those who seek safe shelter from the destroying flames.

A large number of Companies, justly regarded three days ago as perfectly secure, are utterly destroyed, and many others are seriously, **if not fatally, crippled**. Like strong men, they went into the battle, but they now lay dead upon the field of conflict. It remains for those who **survive** to take up the standard and carry it to the front.

Having successfully withstood the calamities and vicissitudes of seventy-seven years, it is a proud satisfaction for the *Old North America*, in this hour of terrible disaster, to bear aloft the Old, Time-honored, and Battle-Scarred Banner, with the assuring inscription thereon of "SECURITY AND INDEMNITY."

But the time has come for a " new departure" in the business of Fire Insurance. During the last two years the downward tendency in **rates**, and increasing demoralization generally, has been very discouraging to Companies of long and varied experience,—Companies that *know that times of unusual disaster must come*, and that unless ample provision is made for same in days of prosperity, total destruction must be the result sooner or later.

Agents and Patrons of the Insurance Company of North America! We must have such compensation for our policies as will enable us, in addition to fair profits to Stockholders, to pay our current losses and expenses, and to lay aside a reasonable percentage of the gross income as a Contingent Fund, to meet such extraordinary losses as have just occurred in Chicago. Let us have this from now and henceforth, and without grudging. An average advance of 25 per cent. will be demanded.

So many companies being " *hors du combat*," you will doubtless have many applications for Policies in the North America, to take the place of others now worthless, and you must be on your guard against too heavy accumulations, and against risks which our rules do not authorize. Report promptly every risk taken, that we may know what we are doing.

Yours very truly,

J. F. DOWNING, GEN'L AGENT.

ERIE, PA., October 10th, 1871.

It is difficult to blame the Insurance Company of North America in Erie, Pennsylvania, for this notice to its agents, sent out on October 10 after heavy losses to insurance firms were evident. A 25 percent increase does, however, seem a bit stiff and, under the tragic circumstances, rather harsh.

PROCLAMATION!

The preservation of the good order and peace of the city is hereby entrusted to Lieut. General P. H. Sheridan, U. S. Army.

The Police will act in conjunction with the Lieut. General in the preservation of the peace and quiet of the city, and the Superintendent of Police will consult with him to that end.

The intent hereof being to preserve the peace of the city, without interfering with the functions of the City Government.

Given under my hand this 11th day of October, 1871.

R. B. MASON, Mayor.

Chicago Historical Society

For some days after the fire and while the city was under martial law, those who wanted to leave the city were given free railroad transportation. Their passes, of which this one issued to Mr. and Mrs. J. Hall is representative, required the signatures of both Mayor Mason and General Sheridan.

On October 11, the day after all of the Great Fire had been quelled, Mayor Mason reluctantly issued this proclamation putting Chicago under martial law. Placed in charge was Lieutenant General Philip H. Sheridan (below, as he appeared while commanding Union troops during the Civil War), who had lived in the city since 1867.

Chicago Tribune

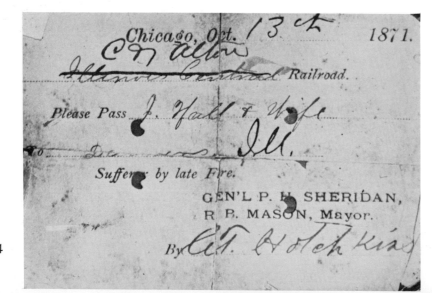

194

Chicago Today

Chicago Historical Society

Waud's on-the-spot sketch of a sentry asking the inevitable question in a city under martial law: "Who goes there?" The occupation by regular and citizen troops was peaceful, except for one tragedy involving Colonel Thomas W. Grosvenor, the city prosecutor who had been foremost among those to demand that Mayor Mason summon uniformed men to maintain law and order. Walking home from a party on the South Side after midnight on October 18, Colonel Grosvenor was challenged by Theodore Treat, a nineteen-year-old University of Chicago student and member of the First Chicago Volunteers recruited for twenty days' service. He refused to reply to the question or to halt. When Treat threatened to fire, Grosvenor yelled, "Go ahead and bang away!" Treat did so and Grosvenor fell, mortally wounded. Carried to his home by firemen from a nearby station, Grosvenor, a contemporary newspaper account reported, "called for his little boy and kissed him goodnight, asked for a glass of water, drank it and died." After protests from Governor John Palmer and rancorous controversy between city and state officials about the use of troops, martial law ended on October 23.

Meanwhile, the task of rebuilding the stricken sector of the city continued. Indeed, even before it proceeded on a full-scale basis, the horsecars were running. This photograph is of the intersection at State and Madison streets looking northeast two days after the end of the Great Fire. Signs on the cars read "West Division Railroad" and "Randolph Street" and "Blue Island Av."

In the midst of rubbish and rubble, a row of seven buildings, headed by a building firm whose name and activity were brightly painted on its white front, was erected on Clark Street north of Lake Street in the week after the Great Fire.

Cornerstone laying for one of the first permanent buildings put up after the fire. The Courthouse and Kerfoot's Block may be seen in the left background.

The Central Union Block, Market and Madison streets, was begun October 16 and finished in two months. It was the first brick block after the Great Fire and later housed, among other tenants, the Illinois Trust and Savings Bank, which was chartered in June, 1873, and survived that year's October panic.

Michigan Avenue above Adams Street, a few weeks after the Great Fire. Those are temporary wooden structures on the east side of the street. Note the freight train leaving town on the lake trestle at top of photograph.

Kogan-Wendt Collection

Around a long-discarded, rusting and empty iron water tank in a lot at La Salle and Adams streets, a temporary City Hall was built. It opened for official business early in 1872 and lasted until 1885. Because of the inordinately large number of pigeons it attracted, it became known as the Rookery, a name later affixed to an office building on the same site which has endured for many years as one of Chicago's famed architectural landmarks.

Kogan-Wendt Collection

In the months after the Great Fire, one of the most notable and important contributions to the city was some 7,000 volumes donated by various countries but principally from Great Britain by such dignitaries as Queen Victoria, Thomas Hughes, Charles Kingsley, John Stuart Mill, Dante Gabriel Rossetti and Benjamin Disraeli and by lesser-known Englishmen. The water tank around which the City Hall had been constructed was refurbished and served to house these volumes in the city's first free public library.

Kogan-Wendt Collection

Many were the city's boosters and boomers, who summoned businessmen and other citizens to a zealous campaign to restore the city. Joseph Medill kept sounding the keynote in his *Tribune,* with editorials stressing the city's future promise: "All is not lost. Though four hundred million dollars' worth of property has been destroyed, Chicago still exists. She was not a mere collection of stones, and bricks, and lumber. . . . We have lost money, but we have saved life, health, vigor and industry. . . . Let the Watchword henceforth be: Chicago Shall Rise Again." Medill was later elected mayor after campaigning on the Union-Fireproof ticket.

Chicago *Tribune*

John Stephen Wright was an editor, author and real estate dealer whose book *Chicago Past, Present and Future* had been published by D. H. Horton. No stranger to adversity, he had failed completely during the Panic of 1837 but had recovered to become prominent among civic leaders. On Monday, October 9, Wright and Horton met at Wabash Avenue and Congress Street amid smoke and flame and ruins, and Horton asked wryly: "What do you think of the future of Chicago now?"

Wright was as undaunted as ever —and prophetic: "I will tell you what it is. Chicago will have more men, more money, more business within five years than she would have had without this fire."

McCormick was one of the great Chicago names, and Cyrus Hall McCormick, who invented the reaper at the age of twenty-two, was one of the best-known owners of that name. Although McCormick had been a resident of New York for several years, he was staying at the Sherman House on the night of the fire. The McCormick Reaper Works and a large amount of his other property were destroyed. But McCormick, with clothing damaged by the flames, met his wife at the railroad station Tuesday morning. Both then went to the factory, where the employees were told that rebuilding would begin as quickly as possible. It did.

Chicago Historical Society

George Frederick Root, whose "From the Ruins Our City Shall Rise!" was a song in true booster-boomer tradition. These lines typified the resurgent spirit:

Dreary, dreary, the darkness falls,
While the autumn winds moan through blackened walls.
But see! The bright rift in the cloud
and hear the great voice from the shore!
Our city shall rise!
Yes, she shall rise!
Queen of the west once more!

Chicago Historical Society

Most evangelistic of the boomers and boosters in the postfire period was Deacon Bross. He brooded hardly at all over the destruction of his home on Terrace Row and wasted no time in heading East, where, as one of the first eyewitnesses, he was interviewed by reporters wherever he went. More important, he visited one banker after another and also called out to all within range of his strident voice: "Go to Chicago now! Young men, hurry there! Old men, send your sons! Women, send your husbands! You will never again have such a chance to make money!" In seeking fortunes, all were now equal in Chicago, cried Bross. "I tell you, within five years Chicago's business houses will be rebuilt, and by the year 1900 the new Chicago will boast a population of a million souls. . . . I know that the location of Chicago makes her the center of this wealthy region and the market for all its products. What Chicago has been in the past, she must become in the future —and a hundredfold more!"

OFFICE OF "THE KIRBY,"
No. 600 SOUTH MORGAN STREET,
CHICAGO, ILL., October 14, 1871.

To OUR AGENTS AND FRIENDS:

GENTLEMEN—The story of terrible destruction by fire in this
from last Saturday night to Monday night, cannot have failed to reach you. We
attempt no description of it. No history will ever be written, no picture ever pai
that will convey to those who did not witness it, more than a faint realization of its
devastation.

We print this on our little press in our own office, as the most available means o
forming you that WE ARE SAFE; that the fire was not in the vicinity of our warehou
and our only losses are through other parties who are sufferers.

We are adding our " mite " to the bounteous charity of the whole world in aid of
suffering, and hope to promptly receive from all who are indebted to us—AND WHO
NOT SUFFERERS— that which is due.

Remittances, for the present, should be made in Currency by Express, Drafts on
York, or in Post Office Orders; as all Drafts on Chicago for a time will need to be
turned, causing great delay, inconvenience and loss of the use of money.

Very respectfully,

D. M. OSBORNE & CO.,
By DANIEL RANSOM.

Chicago Historical S

This is a dunning note, but a thoughtful one. It is addressed to "our agents and friends" by Daniel Ransom of D. M. Osborne & Co., under the date of October 14, and says that while the flames did not damage the Osborne warehouse, the firm hopes to receive "from those who are indebted to us—AND WHO ARE NOT SUFFERERS—that which is due." The notice, incidentally, was printed "on our little press in our own office."

LINES WRITTEN ON THE MOST DREADFUL FIRE
THAT BROKE OUT IN CHICAGO IN AMERICA
COMPOSED BY JERAMIAH CRONAN

YOu simpathising Christians I pray yon' listen unto me
While I relate the dreadfl state of thOusands in America
The fearful fir that has broke out it leaves us all in greif & pain
For the loss of our dear Iri8h freinds alass will never see their hOme
again

On the 7 of October we'll remember it now & for evermore
The dreadful fire that has broke out which cause's thousands of to
deplore
The rageing flames with pains & screams for which we'll weep both
night & day
Most dreadful was their sufferings in Chi oca in America

It was a shocking sight to see those victims young & old
In frightful flames & torturous pains enough to make your blood
ran cold
Mothers Sons & Dauters in thousands they afoud did cry
For mercy & forgiveness unto the Lord that rules on high

When they were leaving Ireland & parting the hOme they landed
dear
Little did their relations think tht this sad news they were doomed
to dear
Their neibours friends & parents who ofte times for them did pray
They are now consum'd in fire in Chfcago all in America

Those who escaped this dreadful doom they claim our pity too
To see tem runing from the fire shouting alas what shall we do
The Mothers with their children it was heartrending for to hear
The screams of them were terifying the hardest heart would shed a
tear

As they suffer'd this most aunl death we hope their souls in heaven
may dwell
The pains & torture they went through I'm sure no mortal tongue
tell
Thei loving friends in Irland will weep for them for many a day
With broken hearts lamen ing their loss by fire in America

Now there has been a noble call through the world every where
To raise up n subscription for the surviving sufferers there
And in every part let each feeling he rt come forward with their mite
For to assist those poor distres'd may God protect them day & night

So now to end these feeling lines I hope y u all will lend your aid
And freely extend your charity to those poor suffering people God has
sav'd
And may you r c ive he reward that has been promised upon the
great a ounting day
And for those poor Ch istians that lost their lives let young and old
now for them pray

P Brereton printer 58 Goose Street Dublin

If this verse, supposedly written by one "Jeremiah Cronan" of Dublin is not a hoax—as some authorities suspect—then Cronan is one of the worst poets who ever lived, even though some of the poor quality may be blamed on an equally incompetent printer. One brief quotation, errors and all:

> YOu simpathising Christians I pray yon'
> listen unto me
> While I relate the dreadfl state of thOusands
> in America
> The fearful fir that has broke out it leaves us
> all in greif & pain
> For the loss of our dear Iri8h freinds alass
> will never see their hOmes again.

Work has begun in earnest on a new Chamber of
Commerce Building at Washington and La Salle streets.
Considerable stimulus for its reconstruction came within
three days after the end of the fire when the members of
the Board of Trade, which had occupied the second
floor of the destroyed structure, passed a resolution
pledging compliance with the original lease and urging
managers of the Chamber of Commerce "to rebuild at
once, as we wish to reoccupy the building at the earliest
possible day." The first stone was laid that November
6, and within a month bricklayers were at work.

Chicago Historical Society

Early in 1872, this much progress had been made on the Chamber of Commerce Building. Its formal opening was on October 9, 1872, with a huge parade, ceremonies and speeches by civic dignitaries including Mayor Medill. The Board of Trade, true to its promise, set up its crucial commercial activities in the handsome structure and remained there until 1885, when it built its own "Temple of Commerce" on Jackson Boulevard and La Salle streets. The Chamber of Commerce Building stood here until the early 1920's.

Chicago Historical Society

Chicago Today

The Field and Leiter wholesale building was another symbol of the city's resurgence. It was rebuilt in 100 days at the corner of Madison and Market streets. Sadly, another local industry also had a quick revival: A year after the Great Fire, Chicago could count precisely 2,218 saloons, one for every 150 inhabitants.

One of the most haunting of postfire photographs shows survivors gathered near the city's Water Tower a mile north of the river as reconstruction begins in the North Division. In the 1880's, when Oscar Wilde visited Chicago, he aroused citizens who doted on the Water Tower's symbolism by referring to it as "a castellated monstrosity."

Chicago *Sun-Times*

An unknown photographer climbed to the top of the
Water Tower seen in the preceding photograph to record this view toward the northwest in the North Division. Most of the debris has been removed, and
rebuilding is well under way.

Another view, looking southeast, from atop the Water Tower in 1872, showing the speed with which the city has sprung to life.

The near North Side, as it appeared in 1873 from the Water Tower, looking northwest. Building here and elsewhere continued its pace in this year despite a financial depression that struck not only the city but the rest of the country and led to inevitable strife between labor and capital. Another huge fire struck the city on July 14, 1874, starting only a few blocks from where the Great Fire had its origins and devastating an area with 800 buildings, mostly frame, with eventual losses amounting to $3,000,000.

The Grand Pacific Hotel finally opened in 1873 after being rebuilt by John B. Drake at the corner of Clark Street and Jackson Boulevard for $1,500,000. Among guests at the ornate establishment shortly after the opening was the King of the Sandwich Islands.

Kogan-Wendt Collection

When the magnificent Palmer House was threatened by flames during the Great Fire, John Mills van Osdel, its architect, collected his construction plans, record books and blueprints and buried them all in a pit in the hotel's basement, covering the hole with two feet of sand and a thick layer of damp clay. After the holocaust they were re-covered undamaged, a discovery that later led to the use of clay tile for fireproofing. Here is the new Palmer House as it appeared in 1875, the city's largest hotel at a cost of $3,500,000. It stood at State and Monroe streets until 1925, when the present Palmer House equally impressive but less opulent, replaced it.

The famed Palmer House barbershop, its marble floor inlaid with silver dollars. Equally renowned was the hotel's elegant grand parlor and its several dining rooms which featured buffalo, antelope, bear, mountain sheep, boned quail in plumage, partridge and other "ornamental dishes."

Fred Townsend Collection

Before 1871 ended, a number of prominent Chicagoans—Potter Palmer and Cyrus McCormick among them—proposed construction of an exposition hall that would not only be useful for conventions and displays but would symbolize the city's determination to rise from adversity. The result was the Interstate Industrial Exposition Building on Michigan Boulevard, completed in 1873, in which year an industrial fair drew 60,000 visitors. The building is at the right, with three cupolas, facing the Illinois Central tracks and Lake Michigan.

A front view of the Exposition Building in the late 1870's, showing the extensive use its architect, William W. Boyington, made of glass. Although rent was free, the industrial expositions ran up deficits for a number of years. When a slight profit was finally reached, the city's aldermen demanded payment of an annual rental. "They did not appear to understand," wrote A. T. Andreas, "how it was that a number of wealthy people banded together in corporation can be thoroughly unselfish, public-spirited and philanthropic."

An interior view of the Exposition Building from one of the exhibit catalogues. Many Chicagoans thought of the building as the city's Crystal Palace. In addition to the yearly industrial shows, it served a multitude of other events, ranging from concerts by Theodore Thomas and the Chicago Symphony Orchestra to the Republican and Democratic conventions of 1884. The building was torn down in 1891 to make way for the imposing Art Institute.

A symbol of postfire affluence. Perry H. Smith, an attorney and politician, built this mansion on the near North Side in 1874 at a cost of $200,000. It included a ballroom, a private theater and a gleaming kitchen, whose unequaled feature was a trio of faucets—one for cold water, one for hot water and one for iced champagne. In the 1880's Potter Palmer daringly constructed a massive Gothic-style castle on Lake Shore Drive amid mud and frog ponds. Fellow millionaires scoffed at him, but within months after his mansion was finished property values in the surrounding area rose more than 150 percent. Palmer's castle stood there for more than six decades before its demolition to provide a site for a complex of apartment buildings.

By 1875, Wolf Point, a spit of land in the Chicago River at Franklin Street that had been scourged by flames four years earlier, was a bustling site for lumberyards and grain elevators and for docks for tall-masted ships. In that same year, some $30,000,000 worth of new theaters, railroad stations, office buildings, mansions and churches went up in the areas most heavily attacked in the Great Fire.

Chicago Historical Society

Long after the Great Fire ended, public interest still ran high. In addition to the famous and profitable Gross Cyclorama, various pictorial and theatrical presentations were staged. This advertisement is for a production in 1878 which, to judge from some of the panels—especially the barroom shooting and the lamppost lynching while soldiers presumably hold off a crowd—was excessively imaginative.

In virtually every decade after the Great Fire, as the city more than bore out the predictions of the boomers and boosters, there arose a new symbol of Chicago's resurgence. This striking photograph by John Szarkowski, now director of the photography department of the Museum of Modern Art in New York, is of a section of Louis Sullivan's famous Auditorium building and theater, topped by the architectural genius' tower, a highly original concept for offices. The Auditorium, a prime example of the city's era of architectural vitality and innovation, opened in 1889. The building still stands, housing Roosevelt University, and the theater, after years of campaigning by zealous Chicagoans, has been restored to original grandeur.

Kogan-Wendt Collection

Even more representative of the city's determination to display to the world its progress since the Great Fire was the winning of the right to stage a multimillion-dollar fair commemorating the four hundredth anniversary of Columbus' discovery of America. In 1893, Chicago played host to hundreds of thousands of visitors at the World's Columbian Exposition. This view shows the Agricultural Building and the Machinery Hall on the left and the elaborately fashioned McMonnies Fountain on the right.

On the morning of October 10, 1871, the corner of Dearborn and Randolph streets, in the city's business section, lay devastated and forlorn, still covered by a pall of smoke. An intriguing contrast is shown in this 1910 photograph of a traffic tie-up at the same intersection.

Again, a vivid contrast. The Great Fire swept almost everything away at this corner of State and Madison streets. This 1922 photograph shows what Chicago chauvinists have always considered "the world's busiest corner" in the days of one of its most flamboyant mayors, William Hale "Big Bill" Thompson, whose banners touting his Pageant of Progress Exposition sway above the State Street traffic.

Kaufmann & Fabry

Chicago *Sun-Times*

An aerial view of yet another event in postfire decades that inevitably prompted recollections and comparisons with the Great Fire and its effects. On the city's official hundredth birthday in 1933, the Century of Progress Exposition was staged on two islands along the lakeshore, featuring, among many wonders, fascinating industrial and scientific exhibits, avant-garde architecture, a Skyride with rocket cars, the Jehol Temple whose gold-leaf exterior was worth more than $25,000, and a lady named Sally Rand, who danced in the nude strategically covered by two feathered fans.

Chicago *Sun-Times*

In 1937, *In Old Chicago,* a Twentieth Century-Fox movie, was climaxed by a rip-roaring depiction of the Great Fire. Much of the basic story was fictionalized. Alice Brady, playing Mrs. O'Leary, was presented as the owner of a French laundry and the mother of two sons, one the city's mayor (Don Ameche) and the other an underworld gambler (Tyrone Power). Actually, the O'Learys had five children, and one son, "Big Jim" O'Leary, did become a gambling boss, achieving fame as head of a syndicate that controlled some 600 handbooks and betting rooms on the South Side and dying a millionaire in 1926. Above, Miss Brady, who won an Academy Award as best supporting actress that year, is rescued after she is trapped in the midst of a frenzied crowd. Below, she, Power and Alice Faye, as Power's sweetheart, sit in a wagon in the cooling Lake Michigan waters with the blazing city in the background.

Chicago *Sun-Times*

Chicago *Daily News*

For years, Chicago's Fire Prevention Week, complete with fire-fighting displays, lectures and demonstrations on safety and parades of old-style equipment, has begun every October 8. In this photograph taken in the 1940's, an ancient horse-drawn steamer goes down a historic thoroughfare—De Koven Street—and past the building, on whose stairs stands a throng of spectators, that was then on the site of the O'Leary cottage and barn.

Two markers installed by the Chicago Historical Society—the first in 1881, the second in 1937—on the De Koven Street building are shown at right. Interestingly, although most authorities, including the late H. A. Musham, without question the most scholarly and knowledgeable expert on the subject, have agreed that the fire did start in the O'Leary barn after a cow kicked over a lamp, the second of the markers concluded: "Although there are many versions of the story of its origin the real cause of the fire has never been determined." Building and plaques are gone now. The picture below shows the building being demolished in 1956 to make way for the Chicago Fire Academy, a sleek and modern training school for city firemen.

Chicago Today

Chicago *Sun-Times*

227

Another 100-years-later photograph by Winek of a section attacked by the Great Fire. The scene is looking east toward Lake Michigan along the Chicago River and flanking areas. The cylindrical buildings in the left foreground are the Marina Towers, and to their right and toward the rear other lofty apartment and office high-rises.

William Winek

Nearly a century after the Great Fire, a remarkable Chicago photographer in his early eighties, William Winek, took his specially constructed panoramic-lens camera to the roof of the Fire Academy and aimed it northeast, recording the area that was destroyed in the holocaust, with the present Loop business district in the background.

William Winek

William Winek

William Winek

And finally: Two panoramic photographs attesting to Chicago's ultimate physical reconstruction. At left, the view is south from the city's loftiest skyscraper apartment building near the junction of the Chicago River and Lake Michigan. Below, from the same site looking north, the scene encompasses the famed lakeshore business and residential district—highlighted by the John Hancock Center, one of the world's tallest buildings with its twin television towers—and the crowded vastness to the northwest. For all their exuberant prophecies, even Joseph Medill and Deacon Bross and John Stephen Wright and all the boosters and boomers of a century ago would be astonished—but immensely pleased—at what has been wrought in those 100 years since Chicago was ravaged by the Great Fire.

Index

Figures in italics refer to photographs.